NO NEW
MORALITY

NO NEW
MORALITY

*Christian Personal Values
and Sexual Morality*

DOUGLAS RHYMES

CANON LIBRARIAN OF
SOUTHWARK CATHEDRAL

THE BOBBS-MERRILL COMPANY, INC.
A Subsidiary of Howard W. Sams & Co., Inc.
Publishers • Indianapolis • Kansas City • New York

CONTENTS

To my Mother and Betty

NO NEW MORALITY

A BASIS FOR
CHRISTIAN ETHICS

One

The present controversy

"To preach morality is easy," said Schopenhauer, "to find a foundation for morality is hard." It is that very task which has become a pressing urgency today. One group after another has questioned the whole foundation upon which morality is based—at first from outside the Church, with the questionings of writers, dramatists, psychologists, existentialist thinkers—and now from within the Church itself.

From Cambridge Harry Williams and Donald MacKinnon question the very foundations on which traditional Christian morality has been built: Williams maintains, both in *Soundings*[1] and in *Objections to Christian Belief*,[2] that much of what passes for Christian morality is simply trying to live up to what is quite unreal to the true self: "A great deal of what Christians often call virtue on closer inspection turns out to be cowardice."[3] Paul Tillich speaks of the moral law too intolerable to be borne. The Bishop of Woolwich criticises the idea of moral laws which "come down direct from heaven and are eternally valid for human conduct."[4] The group of Quakers who drew up the document *Towards a Quaker View of Sex*[5] say "we reject almost completely the traditional approach of the organised Church to morality with its supposition that it knows precisely what is right and wrong, that this distinction can be made in terms of an external pattern of behaviour and that the greatest good will come only through universal adherence to the pattern."

The protest which is being made on all sides is no new protest. It is a protest against a theory of moral conduct which is rooted in obedience to a law. There have always been two main views of ethics: that goodness consists in obedience to a law—be it the law of reason, the law of nature, the law of duty or the law of God—or that goodness consists in the fulfilment of a certain end, as, for example, the Marxist view of ethics.

There is a third view, which is that goodness is determined by the adequacy with which an individual is to live his life in its wholeness, so that the goodness of an action is determined by its place in the scheme of life of a person; that what is good and right is what provides for the deepest welfare of a particular person in a particular situation. To this view I will return later.

First, let me return to the controversy as it affects the Christian view of morality. The attack which is being made within the Church starts from the assumption that the basis of Christian morality as taught by the Church is essentially a law-basis, and asserts that this is not a true interpretation of Christian moral teaching. We must then first examine the assumption and decide whether or not it is correct, and, secondly, ask the question: "Is a moral code based upon a law really the teaching of Christ?"

Is Christian morality based upon law?

There is no doubt that the whole inheritance of Judaism into which Christianity came was an inheritance of a legalistic moral system. God

had laid down certain commandments which
were delivered to Moses, and those commandments had eternal validity because they carried
with them the ultimate authority of God Himself. It is on the basis of these commandments
that every action must be judged, and in the
Book of Leviticus a complicated system of rules
is laid down covering almost every sphere of
human action. "This shall be" and "This shall
not be" becomes the code by which human conduct is directed and judged, and for the regulation of sexual conduct the most detailed rules
are laid down.

This attitude of obedience to the law became
more and more onerous, until by the time of
our Lord practically nothing could be done even
as an act of mercy without some disobedience
to the law. The Priest and the Levite would be
defiled if they touched the wounded Samaritan;
the taxgatherer and the prostitute were people
with whom one could have no sort of associa-
tion; healing on the Sabbath Day must be
frowned upon. In fact, St. Paul found it quite
impossible to live by the law, and for him that
which was meant to regulate good living became
instead an occasion of living death: "And the
commandment which was ordained to life, I

found to be unto death. For sin, taking occasion by the commandment, deceived me, and by it slew me."[6]

It was this very inheritance of legalism which trapped even the newly converted Jewish Christians of the early Church. To them, if a Gentile became a Christian he had to conform to their laws of morality and of convention; he had to be circumcised, to refrain from eating meats which had been offered in sacrifice, to regard certain foods as unclean, in fact to be a Jew under the law as well as a Christian. It is against this legalistic attitude that St. Paul passionately declaims when he urges the Galatians: "with freedom did Christ set us free: stand fast, therefore, and be not entangled again in a yoke of bondage."

Yet it is very difficult to get away from an environment which has heavily stressed the law, and this is a difficulty which one is constrained to feel St. Paul never overcame. His whole attitude to morality is still an attitude of legalism, of a legalism which sees two laws operating in a dynamic hostility—the lower law of the flesh and the higher law of the spirit. This enmity of the flesh and the spirit is something peculiar to St. Paul. In the Old Testament the word "flesh" means the entire human being: in Psalm 16, verses 9ff., heart, glory, soul and flesh mean the whole man in different manifestations, and there seems little suggestion that there is enmity between the flesh and the spirit—rather are they within the one scale of existence of the individual with the outward manifestation, the flesh, of the inward, the soul. Nor in the Gospels do we find this division between the flesh and the spirit as laws warring against each other: all flesh means either all souls within bodies of flesh or an expression of community of soul as "the twain shall be one flesh." In the famous passage of St. John the normally weak flesh is regarded as the perfect embodiment of the divine Logos; this was the scandal to both Jew and Greek—"the word became flesh and dwelt amongst us"; and in the important passage of John 6, verses 51-56, the flesh and blood of Jesus means Jesus himself in his totality: to eat his flesh and drink his blood means to take in his life.

But to St. Paul the flesh is distinguished from the body: it is not part of the whole man. The flesh is man as he has allowed himself to become in contrast with man as God meant him to be. The flesh stands for human nature weakened, vitiated and tainted by sin. Now it is true that there is a conflict in the soul of man—a conflict between himself as he is meant to be and himself as he has become, and this conflict finds expression both in the Old Testament and in the teaching of Christ—but when St. Paul regards this as a conflict between two laws—the law of the flesh and the law of the spirit, implying a dualism in the very nature of man—he would seem to be caught up in a mixture of the Jewish legalism (the notion of laws) and the Greek division between body and spirit. The evil of the body occurs time and time again in Greek thought: Philolaus speaks of the body as a "house of detention." Epictetus says the "soul is shackled to the body." Seneca speaks of the "detestable habitation of the body" and both Plato and Philo have this idea of the dualism of man as a soul fettered to a body and brought down by a body.[7] Is it not likely, therefore, when we consider that Paul was a product of both Jewish religion and Greek learning and that Philo was a near contemporary of his and a bridge between Jewish and Greek thought who had great influence on Christian thinking, that this dualism of flesh and spirit is an inheritance of both Jewish and Greek contempt for the body?

In fairness it must be said the St. Paul does not associate "flesh" only with sexual sin but as the condition of man which lets in all sin, but it is this fatal distinction between the flesh and the spirit and the hostility between them which has so firmly embedded itself in the whole subsequent attitude of the Church to sexual morality and has led to the narrowing down of Paul's view of the flesh to mean what are now normally called "fleshly," i.e. sexual sins. Had we not had his teaching, we might well have had the more Johannine theology that flesh and spirit are man in his totality, a whole being set in relationship to God and to be encouraged to see himself not as a dualism but striving towards that wholeness which in Christ he can find.

The passage which most clearly expresses this hostility between the law of the flesh and the law of the spirit is Romans 7, verses 22-25: "For I delight in the law of God after the inward man: but I see another law in my members warring against the law of my mind, and bringing me into captivity to the law of sin which is in my members. O wretched man that I am! who shall deliver me from the body of this death? I thank God through Jesus Christ our Lord. So then with the mind I myself serve the law of God;

but with my flesh the law of sin." This not only seems to colour the whole of St. Paul's own teaching on marriage and virginity but has consistently coloured the attitude of the Church from age to age: in the heresy of the Manichees, who because of this dualism felt it to be unimportant what was done with the body; in the severe monasticism of the Egyptian hermits. In the elevation of virginity by the Roman Catholics and the elevation of marriage by the Protestants there is, paradoxically enough, almost the same dualism—the flesh is lower and dangerous, so must be forsworn for true holiness, or the flesh is lower and dangerous and must be channelled as harmlessly as possible by the legalised permission of marriage.

I am not for one moment suggesting that there is not some truth in this opposition of flesh and spirit if it be regarded as simply an opposition of will and desire; but if it be regarded, as undoubtedly it has been regarded, as a suggestion that there is something inherently sinful in the activities of the flesh, then I think this is to deny the whole meaning of the Incarnation—"the word became flesh" that the wholeness of the flesh and the person might be seen clearly by all men, and that there might be no sense of guilt or of a lower law in the activities of the flesh. Man is not a dualism of the lower and the higher. Man is a whole being set in relationship to a whole being, subject not to conflict between two laws but to relationship with the ground of his being who is God mirrored in Christ, and to responsible relationships—of flesh and spirit, where both are equally good and necessary— with other beings with whom he realises the love which is the root of his existence.

Williams speaks of the Pharisee thus: "He attempted to make himself and others good by using God and the Law as an ally for the self which he could control and organise by conscious acts of will. This maintained and increased a division in the personality."[8] When St. Paul speaks of the mind serving the law of God but the flesh the law of sin this seems to be a perpetuation of just this attitude. The fact that St. Paul would regard as the ally his relationship with Christ rather than the Law of Moses does not alter the initial premise that man is a divided personality in which one half must keep the other half under control.

This same attitude of St. Paul affects his understanding of marriage, which is dealt with at length in 1 Corinthians 7: "Now concerning the things whereof ye wrote unto me: it is good for a man not to touch a woman, nevertheless, to avoid fornication let every man have his own wife and let every woman have her own husband . . . for I would that all men were even as I myself . . . but if they cannot contain let them marry: for it is better to marry than burn." It has been argued, one suspects by Christians who are embarrassed by these words of St. Paul, that this was written only because of the early expectation of the Second Coming and the necessity of being free to give full attention to the work of evangelism. It is not, I think, possible to say that this is the only reason, for here is simply the logical extension to marriage of the view that there is a dualism in man of which the flesh is the lower part. Moreover, if this were solely an ethic for a particular situation it would be difficult to explain why it has continued, for centuries afterwards, when there was no early expectation of a Second Coming, to be regarded as the basis both for teaching on virginity and celibacy and for teaching on marriage. Dr. Sherwin Bailey, writing of earlier centuries, says: "The general impression left by the Church's teaching upon simple and unlearned people can only have been that the physical relationship of

the sexes was regarded by religion as unworthy, if
not shameless and obscene. The effect of such
teaching must necessarily have been grave; it
caused a distortion of principles and values which
has left an indelible mark upon Christian sexual
thought and we can only guess at the psychological disturbance and conflicts which it has pro-
duced in the lives of individuals."

If it be indignantly denied that this is how
Christians have viewed sexual activity, how do
we explain the fact that until comparatively recently (1928) the marriage service in the official
Prayer Book of the Church of England echoes
the very words of St. Paul: "Secondly, it was
ordained for a remedy against sin, and to avoid
fornication: that such persons as have not the
gift of continency might marry, and keep themselves undefiled members of Christ's body?"
How else do we explain the centuries when
celibacy was exalted as a higher state of man,
and the many people who will feel now that
somehow a man who becomes a monk or a woman who becomes a nun are holier people than
those who exercise their sexuality in marriage?
(Not that religious people themselves take this
view, but it is a popular conception.) Casserley
writes in *The Bent World*: "It must be admitted

that both asceticism and puritanism have con-
spired together to obscure the Christian doctrine
of sex and marriage. The ascetic doctrine of
marriage sees clearly that marriage is good, but
nevertheless tends to relegate it to the realm
of the second best. The general tendency of
puritanism is to regard sexuality as somehow unclean *per se* and to treat marriage, the one per-
missible form of sexuality, as a kind of concession
to the fallen flesh. Under a puritanical regime
almost everyone gets married, but always with
a latent sense of guilt and shame lingering in the
background, because of the puritanical feeling
that sexuality and its characteristic joys are
tainted and unclean."[9]

Without this view of sexuality, perpetuated
through centuries by so-called Christian teaching, would there still be the peculiar embarass-
ment that still besets many parents in teaching
their children about sexual facts? Would there
have been the sense of guilt that still besets much
sexual feeling? Would there have been the opportunities for exploitation by press, films and
novels had there not been this sense of something
delightful but naughty in the very idea of sex?

C. S. Lewis says that something has gone
wrong with the sex instinct, but is it not that

something has gone wrong with the whole attitude of the Curch toward sexual morality, an
attitude which arises from this legalistic morality
of two laws—the law of the flesh and the law
of the spirit warring against each other—an attitude for which St. Paul, not Christ, must take the
blame? It is strange that the Church should seem
to have paid more attention to St. Paul than to
Christ Himself, for there is no trace of this
dualism in His teaching. He never exalts virginity over marriage, except in one instance for
a specific reason—to be utterly free for the work
of the kingdom—and He never suggests that
sexuality is undesirable or a lower level of life.
As the Quaker group says: "a distorted Christianity must bear some of the blame for sexual
disorders of society."[10] Even the words used by
St. Paul carry an implication that has marked
so much of Church thinking: "gift of continency." Why is this a gift? Unless it is presup-
posed that not to have the so-called gift is a mark
of the weaker brethren! It is true, of course, that
there are many Christians today who would not
accept St. Paul's views on this or on many other
things (such as the status of women), but it
cannot be denied that his views have had a great
effect on the Church's teaching regarding both

sexual morality and the general view of society.

The answer, then, to our first question as to whether traditional Christian morality is based upon a law system of ethics is clearly "yes"; it is an authoritarian morality, a system in which certain things are declared to be right and others wrong; it is a matter of rules within which we are supposed to move with absolute conformity, avoiding what we are taught are sins and seeking what we are taught are virtues. We are to obey these rules because they are the laws of God and they have ultimate validity. So often, though, the standard is an external standard rather than a standard of personal responsibility.

We are told that all sexual experience outside marriage is wrong, but we are given no particular rulings about sexual experience within marriage. Yet a person may just as easily be treated as a means to satisfy desire and be exploited for the gratification of another within marriage as outside it. It is strange that we concern ourselves so much with the morality of pre-marital and extra-marital sex, but seldom raise seriously the question of sexual morality within marriage. The rules are hard and fast. While we may and do have compassion for the individuals who cannot keep the law, we have nothing else to offer

but the law. (The Church says there must be
no divorce and remarriage whatever the circumstances.) The laws regarding sexual behavior
are the laws which know no extenuating circumstances. Why? Because they are the laws of God
which have come down through the history of
the Jews, and because of certain sayings of Christ
and of St. Paul which are taken (apparently—
I shall have more to say on this later) at their
most literal value and applied rigorously in this
sphere.

The interesting and ironic thing is that there
are many other explicit sayings in the teaching
of Christ and of St. Paul which are not taken so
rigorously: "turning the other cheek," forgiveness until seventy times seven," "how hardly
shall they that have riches"—to name only a few
of the sayings of Christ—have not been given
force of law that has been given to the sayings
about divorce. St. James has some very explicit
things to say about the respect paid to the rich,
which have been conspicuous by their neglect in
the treatment accorded in the majority of
Churches to the rich and influential. St. Paul
has some words about taking people to court
which have never received the force of law in
the Christian Church! One would have thought

that those who are shocked by what is called "the new morality" would have been equally shocked by Hiroshima or by the recurrence of nuclear testing with its infinite possibilities of physical and mental harm to future generations of children.[11] (The sternest words ever uttered by Christ were against those who harmed children—but even the law of England carries heavier penalties for offences against property than for offences against children!) One would expect protest from the Church about the moral enormity of the homeless, herded together in institutions in London. What many of us find difficult to understand is not that society and the Church have found good reason to cavil at some of the extreme demands of the Gospel, and have found extenuating and existential circumstances why the words of Christ and of St. James cannot be literally applied, but that no extenuating circumstances can ever be found for the breaking of the sexual laws.

The objection, then, which many would rightly make to the authoritarian ethic of the traditional code is that the grounds of its authority are by no means as ultimately valid as is assumed; that to assume that God speaks authoritatively through the legal codes of Leviticus for all time and in all places is to impose an arbitrary limitation upon the nature of God; and, equally, that to make a selection of certain sayings of Christ or of St. Paul and apply them as rigid law for all men is to be dishonest. To suggest that certain sayings should be taken more literally than others for no special reasons of Biblical research, but because a more serious view is taken of sexual sin than of other sin, is to impose not a God-given law but a man-selected law in the name of God.

The reason for this selection lies very largely in the dualistic view of man which has come down through the ages, and to which I have already referred. H. A. Williams says: "The weapon with which the churches bludgeon me on to the broad way is that of inflating the feelings of guilt which lie latent in us all. Make a person feel guilty enough and he will do what he is told."[12] Yes, it is true that we have feelings of guilt. It is natural that we should have feelings of guilt for our lack of response to the love of God, for our failures to exhibit love in our relationships with our fellow-men, for our irresponsibilities and our pathetic attempts to steal from others to make up for the inadequacies of ourselves. But why is this guilt-feeling so strikingly and insistently linked, and encouraged by the Church to be linked, with sexual misconduct? Why is it that we will feel more ashamed over one act of sexual immorality than over a dozen acts of lack of charity? Why does the *Church Times* feel constrained to be more outraged over "the new morality" than over "the old morality" of business chicanery, sharp practice, expense lunches, class snobbery and false national prestige? Why this singling out of one of the seven deadly sins upon which alone the Church is to loose its thunderbolts and make its rigid rules?

Is it not because there has been perpetuated this sense of guilt about the sexual nature of man? As long as we think that we are creatures of a lower nature, which is the flesh, and a higher nature, which is the spirit, then we shall naturally feel guilty about the exercise of the lower nature and pretend to ourselves that we must live up to what we are pleased to call our higher nature, even though this may mean living a pretence and acting a part which is not really ourselves at all. It is when we see ourselves as a whole—a whole which is to be loved for its wholeness, not divided into higher and lower—that we begin to love ourselves, to love the flesh, the mind and the

spirit, because the flesh, the mind and the spirit
are me, and the more I know about myself, the
more I respect myself. The less I feel guilty in
myself, the more I shall respect, know and love
others. There is no part of me for which I need
feel guilty; the only guilt I need feel is when I
have ceased to be myself and, at the command of
someone else, be it priest, Church, politician or
parent, am pretending to be what I am not, and
calling it good.

This long-standing traditional morality, based
upon authoritarian law and suspicion of the flesh,
is today being rejected on all sides, and especially
among the younger generation. Of this there
can be no doubt. For long the state has parted
company with the Church over the matter of
divorce and remarriage, and by far the greater
number of people are with the state rather than
the Church. Now the young are beginning to
react against even the conventional moral standards upheld by their parents, upheld often for
purposes of convention and respectability rather
than for any deep-seated moral motives. Since
only a very small percentage of the nation have
any real allegiance to the Church, it is not sur-
prising that the laws of the Church should not

seem to be binding on those who do not accept
the divine imperative which, it is claimed, lies
behind those laws. Such reasons, for example,
as are given by most parents for the observance
of sexual restraint are reasons which are quite
pragmatic—based more upon fear of the conse-
quences and of loss of status in the community
if anything goes wrong, than upon any concept
of Christian morality. It is even doubtful
whether many of the young within the Church
pay more than lip-service to what is preached
there. I know that in the Youth Clubs with
which I came into contact as a parish priest there
was little regard either for the authority of parents or of priests when it came to the decisions
they made about their own sexual experiences.

This is not to say that there are no moral
standards, or that what is required is a free-for-
all standard without restraint or respect. It implies rather a deep-rooted rejection of authority
simply as authority. What many of the more
thoughtful young people are looking for is a
standard which will make sense and which will
work; they refuse to feel guilty about what seems
to them to involve no necessity of feeling guilty.
In May, 1963, *New Society* made a survey to
try to discover what sort of people we are, and

what kind of Britain we would like to see. The conclusions arrived at by R. P. Kelvin, who conducted this research, are an interesting comment on contemporary personal values: "The detailed analysis of the concept of greatness suggested that moral value in the past was based on the conformity of behaviour to the standards set by the Christian tradition; today however the moral duty of the individual is seen to lie less in conforming to such generally accepted standards than in realising his potentialities as an individual. The Christian tradition is no longer taken for granted . . . our replies imply widespread doubt about the ability of traditional Christian morality to provide moral and religious leadership; and this in turn implies that at the present time there is little confidence in a morality based upon conformity to generally accepted *absolute* standards . . . the moral worth of an individual is seen to rest on his achievements as an individual rather than on his comparative success in conforming to some absolute standards. There is an implicit denial here of the right to judge or be judged, and it is perhaps significant that a majority of those under 40 were biased towards ending all legal interference in private morality rather than towards more positive moral and religious leadership. The great majority of all ages favoured divorce by consent, and in effect opposed the existing laws which strongly reinforce conformity to a religious tradition in the solution of an essentially private and personal problem." Kelvin goes on to say: "personal values and the criteria of moral value thus seem to be undergoing change; not in the direction of amorality and permissiveness, but towards emphasis on the individual's integrity rather than on his conformity to generally accepted absolute standards. Religion is not incompatible with this, but is also seen as not essential to it; and there is quite clearly lack of confidence, albeit often with regret, in the future of the traditional forms of Christian morality."[13]

I have given this rather long quotation because here is the result of a scientifically conducted sociological survey, and not just the expression of personal opinion—a survey which, nevertheless, bears out what has become increasingly obvious: that authoritarianism as such, if pursued, will be heeded by less and less of the maturing generation.

The other reason for the rejection of traditional morality has been clearly developed by H. A. Williams and others who follow his think-

ing. The development of psychological understanding has led to deeper self-knowledge, to a
realisation that fullness of living demands an
awareness of the full self and a release of its in-
nate powers for the business of living. As Hei-
degger, the existentialist philosopher, has argued,
man is a being of concern or care and he is confronted by death. His problem is to find a significant existence in the face of these limitations. He
finds this significant existence, the psychologist
would state, not by trying to subject one part of
himself, the flesh, to another, the spirit, but by
finding the whole self, accepting the whole self,
and in that awareness living not by law but by
the liberty of the freedom he has found.

The freedom found in Christ

So we pass to our second study. Traditional
morality is rejected. If that traditional morality
is the morality of Christ, then the rejection might
well be a cause of sadness; but we, as Christians,
should have to hold to that morality however
few accepted it. The Church press accuses H.A.
Williams, the Quakers and the Bishop of Wool-

wich of undermining basic Christian teaching
and flying in the face of the witness of Christ.
If this were true—if it is true that the traditional
moral code is in fact the teaching of Christ, then
whatever the world's attitude we should have to
hold fast to that code, for right is not made wrong
by popular opinion. But the much more vital
question is: Is this the teaching of Christ? Is the
moral code of an authoritarian and unvarying
law, is the dualism of flesh and spirit, really the
teaching of Christ, or have we to rethink our ethical teaching, and discover anew the mind of
Christ for this age? Let us then set about the task
of discovering how Christ Himself deals with
individuals and the standards which He sets before them.

The first thing that we notice is the complete
absence of law in Christ's way of dealing with
people. His attitude is always that the needs of
men come before law, that the law is subservient
to men, not men to the law. This appears
throughout His teaching, and it is for this that
He was continually condemned; He was accused
of having no respect or concern for the law.

He claimed the right to heal on the Sabbath.
To allow His disciples to satisfy their needs of
food in the corn-field was more important than

any regulations. To satisfy His own needs was
of more importance than social custom, as witness
His words to the Pharisee who expressed surprise
that He did not wash before a meal. He said
quite openly that man was not made for the
Sabbath, but the Sabbath for man. When chal-
lenged to deal with the woman taken in adultery
by the method of the law, He scorned the law
and dealt with her, and with those who accused
her, as responsible beings. He spoke scornfully
to those who were concerned with convention:
"You Pharisees! You clean the outside of cup
and plate; but inside you there is nothing but
greed and wickedness."[14] "Did not Moses give
you the Law? Yet you all break it . . . Do not
judge superficially, but be just in your judgements."[15]

It is not that Christ has no respect for codes
and for moral laws, but that He refuses to accept
that there are codes and moral laws which per-
mit of no exceptions. It is the need of man and
the deepest welfare of man which is the first consideration, and this is marked in all His teaching
and in all His dealings with people. He came to
a people burdened with the law, made for ever
guilty by the demands of religion, and unable to
move even in the direction of compassion and

love without being in danger of breaking the law. The Pharisees were not wicked people, or even deliberately hard people, but they could not see that people mattered more than codes; that there was no such thing as a law which was applicable to every person and every situation. Thus, they must protest against Christ, because in Him they found a dangerous spirit of anti-nomianism; a refusal to accept flat laws, however good, as the touchstone by which goodness and morality is measured. So their protest led them into strange paths by which obedience to the rule became more important than concern for the needs of people. So some of us would feel that strange paths have been followed by the opposition of the Church leaders to Mr. Abse's Bill, by which it was considered better that the present burden of squalid evidence of adultery should be the grounds of divorce rather than the proven deadness of a marriage.

It is that burden of rigid obedience to the rule which Christ would want to take from us: "The burden He wants to take from us is the burden of religion. It is the yoke of the law, imposed on the people of His time by the religious leaders, the wise and understanding, as He calls them in their own words—the Scribes and Pharisees, as

they are called usually. Those who labour and
are heavy laden are those who are sighing under
the yoke of the religious law. And He will give
them the power to overcome religion and law;
the yoke He gives them is a 'new being' above
religion. The thing they will learn from Him
is the victory over the law of the wise and the
understanding, and the law of the Scribes and
Pharisees."[16]

It shall be told that the one place where Christ
laid down a definite ruling is in relation to marriage and divorce: I will not say more of that
at present, as that merits much more detailed
treatment in a later chapter. I am concerned
simply to show that the whole tenor of His
teaching was not to further the law, or even to
substitute another law of His own, but to "fulfil
the law"—that is, to concern Himself with fulfilment in the life of man rather than with codes
and regulations.

Why does He concern Himself with people
rather than with law? Because He knew men,
and He knew that men are all different and need
different treatment. This is conspicuous in all
His dealings with individuals. Not all are dealt
with alike. There is no flat law which is given
to each, save the law of love, and the law of reali-

sation of what each can accept and fulfil. So the rich young ruler is called to make complete renunciation of his riches because he has reached the state at which such renunciation could have been possible, and would have removed the last stumbling-block to a life which had already shown a capacity for self-giving love. But He can accept the partial renunciation of Zaccheus —"Behold, Lord, the half of my goods I give to the poor"—without demanding all, because that is as far as Zaccheus can be expected to go after a life-time of believing that money and the exaction of money is all-important. He sees that the woman taken in adultery, and the woman who was a sinner and anointed His feet, needed not social condemnation but restoration and acceptance, because they already felt their guilt and no useful or compassionate purpose would have been served by further condemnation. But He equally saw that the Pharisees needed strong condemnation, because only so could the thick hide of complacency be broken through. He could reason with Pilate because there was that in Pilate, for all his final weakness, which could have responded to justice and truth, but He could not reason with Herod because there was no depth there— nothing but superficiality, before which love can only be silent, and perhaps through silence show up the superficiality for the shallowness that it is. So He deals with people where they are, and leads them on to the next stage of where they can be. Not always do they reach that stage, but it is always within their power to do so, because He will not ask of them what they cannot yet attain and He will not ask of them what is not in them.

His knowledge of man carries Him still farther than this. He will show them what they can be; He will help them to know themselves so that they may love what they know and so learn in the truest sense to love themselves. When Christ asked us to love our neighbors as ourselves He did not mean just that we should give to others the consideration that we are normally accustomed to give ourselves, but something much deeper. We are made in the image of God; God is love; the Incarnation is the revelation of that love in human form. The Incarnation reveals the possibility for every man. We are not meant to regard ourselves as miserable sinners crawling and supplicating at the feet of a capricious God who may, if he feels so inclined, graciously forgive us if we crawl enough. We are meant to regard ourselves as sons of God, as men to whom is given a tremendous responsibility and a tremendous potentiality.

We should be proud of man. Man is a great being. Man is the child of God able to be perfect as his Father in heaven is perfect. Whether man *has* come of age, as the Bishop of Woolwich seems to think, is a debatable point, but he is certainly meant to come of age.

It was said of Jesus that He knew what was in man. He says: "If then the Son sets you free, you will indeed be free."[17] In order to set people free He constantly confronts them with their true selves, with the possibilities which lie within, and that which is blocking those possibilities. He reveals to the Samaritan woman by the well wherein lies the truth which she is concealing from herself by her own pretences. He enables the man born blind not only to see physically but also to see himself truly, and be able honestly to accept God. He shows the woman who is a sinner and who anoints His feet the love that lies within her. He reveals to the centurion his capacity for faith. He mixes with the sinners, the outcasts, because they need not be sinners and outcasts once they have come into touch with love. He is constantly opening the eyes of people to a reality greater than is at present

known to them, so that they may surrender what
they imagine or hope or fear they are to what
in fullness they really are; so that they may not
be guilty about themselves or hide themselves,
but *be* themselves and love themselves. This is
what a legalistic code of morals can never do.
It can only approve the following of a rule, or
disapprove the ignoring of a rule; it cannot call
people to that knowledge of themselves by which
alone the good is possible.

Jesus does not call people to a law; He calls
them to a relationship—a relationship with Himself, who is love, that they may know themselves,
and enter into that same relationship with others.
As Tillich says: "It is not a new demand, a new
doctrine or new morals but rather a new reality,
a new being and a new power of transforming
love . . . forget all Christian morals when you
come to Him. Nothing is demanded of you . . .
only your being open and willing to accept what
is given to you."[18]

Christ calls us then to know ourselves, so that
by knowing ourselves we may learn our responsibility, our love for our neighbour. He calls people to an awareness of their responsibilities in
the situation which is given to them. He does
this often by parable—the responsibility of love

to the wounded Jew on the Jericho road; the responsibility of father to son and brother to brother in the Prodigal Son; the responsibility of Simon to the woman who was a sinner; the responsibility of the men who were stoning the woman taken in adultery to that knowledge of themselves which should have led them to compassion; the responsibility of the disciples to each other, when they were arguing about greatness; and the responsibility of all of them to all men by the feet-washing. He shows the responsibility to works of mercy and healing, the responsibility to know all the facts before pronouncing judgement, and even then to be uneasy about too easy judgement. He shows the responsibility to children; the responsibility of Herod to John the Baptist; the responsibility of the Jew to Caesar; the responsibility of man to wife; of Himself to Mother and to best friend; the responsibility of all men to works of love and compassion as in the parable of judgement.

Christ's standards of dealing with people contain little of law and much of love. He deals with people in their situations and helps them to discover their deepest welfare in that particular situation. He helps them to discover this by revealing to them the possibilities of their own nature and the responsibilities which love lays upon them. His love goes deeper than any law. It goes to the heart of each individual's situation, and it deals with each individual as a separate human being.

It is this attitude to morality which I am seeking. As the Quaker essay says: "the search is a move forward into the unknown . . . it implies a high standard of responsibility, thinking and awareness—something much harder than a moral code." There is a very real sense in which Professor Carstairs' much misunderstood remark is true, for what he said was: "But is chastity the supreme moral virtue? In our religious traditions the essence of morality has sometimes appeared to consist of sexual restraint. But this was not emphasised in Christ's own teaching. For Him the cardinal virtue was charity, that is consideration of and concern for other people."

It seems to me that if Christians approached people with the attitude of Christ rather than with the laws of the Church and the moral code they should be able to reach those who take no notice of the laws of the Church. For there is all the world of difference between approaching a person with a flat law and approaching him with love and concern and understanding in his own situation, and seeking to help him find the best in that situation. The Quakers said, in their television interview, that they started their inquiry because of the way in which society treated homosexuals. Society said, "What horrible people!" They said, "Poor boys, how can we help them?" How much more like the approach of Chist!

We can hope to persuade even the non-Christian that true concern for people involves the acceptance of responsibility for their actions; that true love involves a responsible relationship of love if it is not to end in disaster. We can help him to see that goodness is not just the rather dreary ethical virtues of repression, renunciation, resignation, but the courage to be, the courage to know and love oneself; that herein lies liberty and freedom from slavery, whether to law or to licence.

It will be my task now to work out what this Christ-standard of morality would actually mean in relation to the nature of true love; to dealing with adolescent problems; to marriage and its breakdowns; and to the right judgement of the conduct of others.

LUST OR LOVE?

Two

When I preached a series of Sermons in South-wark Cathedral in March 1963 (which were the origin of this book) I was accused of trying to undermine Christian morality. I would like to state categorically that nothing is farther from the truth. Christian morality is already under-mined in that it is unheeded and rejected by many, and often given lip-service rather than full consent. That is largely because society has the wrong visual image of Christian morality, in that it is thought to be legalistic, oppressive and un-reasonable. The Church must partly bear the blame for this, because it has often been presented as such; presented, I mean, as rule rather than as relationship.

What I am aiming at is not a lower code of morality, but a higher attitude towards the per-son, a personal relationship of responsibility and

of love which will pervade all human relationships; a relationship which will be based not upon
the observance of laws but upon concern for the
person in the situation of the person, and which,
for those of us who are Christians, is rooted in
Christ and His relationship to us.

What we have to face today with greater real-
ism as a Church is that we are living in a secular
society. That this is not necessarily a disastrous
society has been very well brought out by D. L.
Munby in his book *The Idea of a Secular Society*.[1] But that it is there is, he says, something
which cannot be denied. "In effect, for most
important purposes we are a secular society,
where it makes little or no difference in what our
religion or morality consists, and in which
Christians are a small minority. That the State
machinery continues to incorporate archaeologi-
cal fragments appropriate to former periods when
society was Christian is of less importance than
the dominant *mores* of society."[2]

In this secular society are we to have a dual
morality in which a small percentage accept fully
the Christian code so-called, and the rest work
out something quite different for themselves? Or
are we to rethink what the attitude of Christ
means in relation to present-day society, and be

able to train young people so that they may live
in a secular society and yet achieve personal relationships which are not alien to the mind of
Christ? Is there not an ethic where Christians and
humanists can stand on common moral ground?[3]
I believe that even within secular society there is
a consensus on the value and need for stable and
secure family life; on personal values in sex relationships; on the need for the restraint and respect which arise from the understanding of men
and women as whole persons. I believe that if we
carry Christ and His compassion and understanding into the world of those who do not recognise
Him in explicit belief they may yet accept what
He has to give of true freedom and true love.
This is not a new morality, but it is a way of pre-
senting morality which, while entirely in accord
with the mind of Christ and the attitude of Christ,
can win acceptance where the normal attitude
and presentation of the Church has failed.

The contrast between lust and love

In the understanding of personal relationships
the great contrast between the right and wrong

personal relationship lies in the contrast between love and lust; it is often thought that the word "lust" has only a sexual connection, but this is no more true than that the word "love" has only a sexual meaning. The two describe different attitudes towards people, in which there may or may not be involved any sexual action. Williams, in his article in *Soundings*,[4] describes lust as the result of failing to realise our own value, and trying to secure value for ourselves by snatching it from another. In the course of this snatching the physical appetites may or may not be involved. I can never be another person; I can only be myself, and when I try to make another person the instrument of the defects in my own understanding of myself I try to identify myself with that person by some method of behavior which cripples that person or cripples me; and that is lust.

Why should I try to snatch value for myself from somebody else? Basically the reason is that I am insecure, and my insecurity leads me to fear to lose what I already know and have and to try to find the security which I lack myself in the domination or possession of another, as the old verse goes: "How my cabined ego thrives steering other people's lives." It is a "cabined ego" which seeks to do this, not the true ego which has realised itself and can therefore bear that others should be free to realise themselves. That is why it is so important that we should teach people, as did Christ, to be able to see themselves as they are and accept themselves: if we can only see our own insecurity and learn to live with it, rather than snatching from someone else in order to achieve a false sense of security, we should not need to inflict upon others the burdens of our own guilt feelings.

Modern psychiatric treatment is rooted in the healing power of self-awareness. When I have been made aware of the forces which are causing me to act as I do, when I am not afraid of what lies beneath, afraid of the nakedness within, then I can look at myself clearly and learn to be myself and to give expression to what I am without the hurt of another. I am no longer dependent upon someone else to cover my insecurity: I can recognise it for what it is. I can learn to love rather than to lust.

The essence, then, of lust is possessiveness arising from unrecognised insecurity. It takes many forms: many become possessive about their own work, they cling to a job long after their usefulness in that work has gone, because therein lies their security—without that work they

would feel empty, it is the mask which covers
their own emptiness; others become possessive
about their friendships—they cannot bear that
others should share their friends, because their
very friendship is insecure and they are afraid to
lose what they have; others become possessive
about things and their possessions—a housewife
I know spends all her time on her house, to the
extent that it has become a polished museum
rather than a home, this because her relationship
with her husband is insecure and the house to her
is her security; a priest will not allow anything to
happen in his parish without his presence and
wishes to take the lead in everything—this because his own priesthood is insecure and he fears
that if anything is taken away he will not know
how to maintain his status. All these are attempts
to snatch value for myself from somebody else,
the attempt to make that person not themselves
but me—in bondage to me. It is personal relationship at its most harmful, for it means death
to the person I am trying to hold in bondage, and
death to any real attempt to love myself and see
value in myself. It is a parasitic relationship. The
fact that it is sometimes associated with sex is
purely coincidental; and to show that this is so, I
would give you some examples of this kind of

lustful relationship in which there is no specifi-
cally sexual action involved.

A mother says that she loves her son and that
she feels that no other woman can ever care for
him as she has done. The son marries, and the
mother interferes with the marriage, uses every
occasion to belittle the efforts of the wife, constantly reminds the wife of what her son likes and
makes comparisons between what the wife does
for her son and what she used to do. Soon this
may occasion strife between husband and wife,
and it has been known for a wife placed in that
position to leave her husband. Immediately the
mother welcomes him back, says that she always
knew the girl was no good, but she will make her
son happy again. The mother calls this form of
possessiveness love, but there is no love here—
only lust parading as love. Trying to make up for
her own inadequacy as a person, the mother
snatches value for herself through her son.

Or again, a mother is left a widow and there
is one unmarried daughter who now has to give
her life to the care of her mother. The mother
demands the full attention of the daughter, and
any suggestion that the daughter might wish to
marry is resisted by the mother with pleas of:
"Who is going to care for me?" The daughter is

able to have very little life of her own because of
the constant demands of her mother. Even when
she wishes to go out she is met with such talk as
"Of course, I don't wish to stop you, but I do
hope I shall not be taken ill while you are out," or
"Please do not be too long! I don't like being left
in the house on my own." Holidays and associa-
tion with other people become increasingly more
difficult, as the mother cannot stand having
people in the house and cannot be left alone.

One day the mother dies, and the daughter is
left in middle age with her opportunities for marriage gone and her chances of making a real life
for herself at a minimum. The mother has proud-
ly said that her daughter is devoted to her, other
people will applaud the daughter's sacrifice. But is
it to be applauded? Did not the mother in fact
steal the life of her daugher, make her the victim
of her lust, trying to snatch value for herself in
loneliness and old age by taking value from the
daughter?

Here is a third example. A husband is absurdly
jealous of his wife. She cannot speak to another
man or have other friends. She is expected to
react parrot-fashion to his views on everything;
to be his chattel; to carry out his whims and demands. All because he says that he loves her so

much that he cannot bear her out of his sight or
have disagreement between them on anything.
The truth is, of course, that he is not really in love
with her at all. He is destroying the very person
he is supposed to be loving—like the notorious
Mrs. Proudie, of whom it was said, in relation to
her husband: "In the deadly fashion of a master-
ful woman, she is devoted to him." This husband
who talks about love is a creature of lust; he
snatches value from his wife because he is unsure
of himself, and so, to make up for his own inadequacy, he tries to make her into himself.

All these, and many more, are examples of lust;
of relationships which have gone sour. Yet not
one of them is a matter of sexual action. It is an
irony that lust arises from too little, not too much,
self-love. He who is able to love himself is able
to love others also, for he has understood his true
value and does not need to bolster up his own
value by snatching it from others. When I am
unaware of what I truly am I am incapable of
giving myself value, and so I desperately seek
value from someone else; and this leads me to
action which is sometimes identified with sex;
but with sex divorced from its true object, which
is the completion of the union of two people who
have found their own value, and therefore found

value in each other. So the inadequate heterosexual goes in search of the prostitute, the inadequate homosexual in search of the "queer" bar—
because neither knows value in themselves or in
another. How truly did Christ urge us to "love
others as ourselves," knowing that if we really
loved ourselves, that is, knew the value of our
own personality, we should respect and value the
personality of another.

The nature of love

In one sense we have already answered the
question "What is the nature of love?" by contrast with the nature of lust. If I were to be asked
to give a definition of true love I could not do
better than the following quotation from a book
by Vladimir Solovyev, called appropriately *The
Meaning of Love*:[5] "The meaning and worth of
love consists in this, that it effectually constrains
us, in all our nature, to acknowledge for another
the unconditional central significance of which,
in virtue of our egoism, we are conscious only in
our own selves. Love is the transfer of our interest from ourselves to another, as the shifting of

the very centre of our personal life. This is characteristic of every kind of love, but *par-excel-
lence* of sex-love . . . only this love can lead to the
effective and indissoluble fusion of two existences into one; only of it is it also said in the
words of Holy Writ: 'The twain shall be one
flesh', i.e. become one real being."

There are certain requirements, then, of any
relationship which is to exhibit true love:

Love seeks to know. Love validates itself, not
in the blind thrust of an emotion, but in the in-
telligent understanding of the complex mystery
of a human being. This is something about which
we are very bad in the modern world. We want
to put people into categories, to fit them into pre-
conceived patterns; we want in our relationships,
only too often, the immediate sexual satisfaction
before we have taken the trouble to know and to
understand the other person. We do not allow
the significance to the other person that love demands, because we have already decided what we
want, and the other has to fit into what we want.

Love liberates. One of the difficulties that
Marriage Guidance finds is the difficulty which
couples have of making communication with
each other, especially often on the most vital
problems of life. How often does one find this

embarrassment when the deepest problems of life come up. Better to stay on a level where you feel secure, most people think, than to become involved! No one has expressed this better than T. E. Lawrence, whose very life stands witness to a loneliness never assuaged: "There was my striving to be liked so strong and nervous that I could never open myself friendly to another. The terror of failure in an effort so important made me shrink from trying."[6] If only we could be less concerned with the façade which we put before others, less concerned to keep life and conversation at a superficial level; more concerned to be the kind of people with whom others can share things, the kind of people who will liberate the tensions of others because, having seen and faced our own, we can see and face others. We have loved, in the deepest sense, ourselves, and so can see by love the needs of others. For to see is to be able to communicate what is seen.

The freedom which comes from true love is the self-giving which follows the self-seeing, the generous giving of the whole self in love to another, which is why the sex-act is the appropriate outward sacrament of that self-giving. It means in its fullness the giving of all that I am without reserve to all that the other is. If we can only

learn not to hide behind a false self, not to make
a façade, a mask to conceal the real self, but to
seek to know ourselves as fully as possible and not
to feel guilty or ashamed of what we know, then
we can accept what we know, and in that acceptance we can reveal to others and communicate with others. We can learn to give what we
are, not what we think we ought to be. True love
produces chastity without the need of rules, because true love does not proceed from law and
rule, from a pattern to which I conform, but from
the self-knowing and self-giving which is a
matter of body, mind and spirit, a sacrament of
the inner union which I can be.

Love is sacrificial. By that I do not mean the
self-conscious martyrdom, which is simply pretence—"she is the sort of woman who lives for
others, and you can tell the others by their
hunted expression!"—but the sacrifice which
discovers another life which is as dear as our own.
In that realm sacrifice and forgiveness become
meaningful. When the woman who was a sinner
anointed Christ's feet He said: "her sins which
are many are forgiven, for she loved much." All
her life she had been giving herself in the effort to
find love; her first self-giving has been misguided,
for she found that those to whom she gave her

body had no wish to give her significance as a human being, for they had not found it for themselves, and so were incapable of love. When she found Christ she found one who saw her craving for love. The significance that was Himself gave her the significance for which she had been craving. "Just as sacrifice confirms the significance of another human being by giving freely to him or her the full measure of devotion, so forgiveness returns with the gift of communion after another has broken it."[7] We enter a world where we do not condemn but rather seek one another's burdens because we cannot bear them alone.

Let me illustrate what I mean by the requirements of true love in relation to the three examples of possessive lust which I quoted. What difference would it have made to those people had they sought the love which seeks to know, which liberates and which is sacrificial? This mother would have sought first to know herself: she would have recognised in herself the need for the love of the son, and she would have seen that her desire to hold on to him arose from the reassurance of affection she needed. As Tournier says: "There is in the human heart an inexhaustible need to be loved and a continual fear of not being loved. Constantly in all our human rela-

tions and in all our activities, we look for proofs
of love from the other person. We look for them
as remedies for our solitude. We seek others' reassurance. Those who doubt their own worth
have a particularly insatiable desire for marks of
affection because they just as continually doubt
that others could love them."[8] She would by increasing self-awareness see that it is not really
that she loves her son but she is doubting her own
worth and wanting the signs of his love to make
secure the significance of herself. This self-
knowledge would begin the process of liberation
both for herself and for her son: she would then
in the light of the knowledge found of herself
begin to look to his needs. She would see that the
very care she has given him is now to be given by
his wife, and that for the sake of his significance
she must rejoice in this and not grieve over it. It
will be sacrificial: even when she has faced up to
herself and learned to liberate her son, she will
still from time to time yearn to be the one who
gives him the caring and the love rather than the
wife, but she will probably find that the very love
she needs will in fact return to her when she has
freed her son, and she may well discover that
both the son and wife value her the more because
her love is no longer a burden to them. What she

demanded she in fact lost: what she gives she may well find restored.

The exercise of true love in the second example of the mother with the daughter is far more difficult. Here is the problem of old age and the loneliness of old age. It is an increasing problem, because people are living longer. The desire to feel needed, to be of use, to be cherished and loved becomes stronger as old age brings a sense of insecurity about all these needs. Perhaps here it is easier for the single person than for the married: the single know that, however bitter it may be, they have to learn to accept loneliness when they are old, for there will be no family to whom they can become a burden. This is not the case when there is a family, and especially when there is a single daughter, who might reasonably be expected to care for the mother. I am not suggesting for a moment that the care of the old is not a proper care both for the family and for the community as a whole. Nevertheless, it is possible to face up to old age and to be able to recognise and accept that despite our needs we must not become a burden or dominate the lives of those who have a right to their own life. I know of an old lady who firmly refused to live with her children, who knew herself sufficiently well to know that she could not do so without making demands upon them which would hamper them. She put herself into a pleasant and agreeable home for old people, has her own sitting-room there, entertains visitors and because of her cheerful disposition has many; she finds with the others in the home a community which mitigates her loneliness, is regularly visited by her children, who come gladly to see her with no sense of a grim duty, and has found her own happiness and peace, which is easy to see. It is, of course, a great deal easier for this to happen if there are financial resources which make this possible, and it should be the duty of the state to see that there are more of such pleasant homes available in which there can be real comfort and community.

However, it must be faced that for many this self-knowing and liberating love will be truly sacrificial: it may well involve going through a state of despair and desolation until there comes a time when that involvement can be accepted and conquered: it may mean the acceptance that a loving old age can be a lonely old age. Such acceptance, if it is a real acceptance induced by self-awareness, will kill the resentment and the bitterness, and the result will be the peace within which is the healing of old age. As Williams says: "It is thus that I pass through involvement with an alienated self, the cross and the passion, to the glory of the resurrection."[9] For many of us as we grow older there must be the realisation that it is only when we have gone through the feeling of: "My God, my God why hast thou forsaken me" that we are able to arrive at the freedom of: "Father, into Thy hand I commend my spirit."

So with the mother and the daughter in my example the true love of the mother will be that while she may well live with the daughter and be cared for by her, she will be very careful to see that by no words or attitude of her own is the daughter chained: she will learn to accept that she must be on her own, that the daughter must be free to go out, to have her friends, and that should the daughter desire to marry she will rejoice in that fact, learn the acceptance of what it may mean for her and see that any rearrangements are already in her mind so that the daughter does not need to feel guilty. In such a way she will have truly accepted old age and its loneliness rather than seeking to compensate for it by snatching value from her daughter.

The third example of the husband and wife is yet another case of the husband seeking compen-

sation for his own inadequacy: jealousy always
arises from consciousness of insecurity. It becomes a vicious circle because it creates what it
fears. No one can stand being watched, having
such demands made upon them that nothing they
can do can quench them. The more we give way
to the jealous person, the more he will expect; the
more we try to accommodate ourselves to his demands, the more we shall realise that there is no
limit to the demands. So at last there comes the
point when, exasperated beyond endurance, and
unable to be enslaved any longer, the partner demands the right to freedom and so heightens the
other's jealousy.

In all love relationships, whether it be of marriage or of deep friendship, there must be self-
knowledge, freedom and sacrifice: it is unreason-
able to expect that a relationship will provide in
itself all that is necessary to life, however happy
the marriage or friendship may be. There will be
other interests, other friendships and other needs
which must be fulfilled in other directions than
that of the partner. To give significance to another person means to give freedom within marriage for that person's significance to be expressed
through others than the marriage partner, to be
willing to be self-giving because in my own self-

knowing I have come to see myself as I am and so to realise that I cannot fulfil every interest of the one I love. He or she needs sometimes to be away from me, not that I may be less loved, but that I may prove my love: the taking and demanding of love is only one side and the lesser side of love, the giving is the true proof of love. When I am able to rejoice that the one I love sometimes needs others for companionship, then I have learnt the meaning of love. I know a marriage where this is completely understood: the husband knows that there are certain interests of his wife that he cannot fulfil, he gives her the complete freedom to share those interests with others with whom she has them in common, he allows her without a hint of jealousy to make deep friendships which give great satisfaction to her and to her friends; the husband feels that he is deprived of nothing, for he knows himself and his own needs are fully met by her, her other needs do not undermine his security. If he had tried to cut out of her life those needs which are hers, and which he cannot and does not wish to fulfil, he would, perhaps, have lost her full love; by giving her freedom learnt through self-awareness he has retained her deepest affection and strengthened greatly his own marriage.

This is, of course, not easy. It is much easier to lust than to love; much easier to make demands and call it love than to give love. To love is always to be vulnerable to hurt. Love costs and may be rejected. Because of our insecurity, of our lack of self-awareness, we fear to love and prefer to lust—to demand affection. This demand will also and even more certainly bring rejection, because the demands become intolerable and kill what love was there. But there is a difference between the loneliness which follows the rejection of the true self-giving love and the loneliness which follows the demanding love: the former learns the value and meaning of love, the latter learns only bitterness and self-pity. Christ on the Cross was rejected, and through that rejection men found the life of love which casts out fear. There is much to learn of love in the prayer of St. Francis: "Let me not seek to be consoled as much as to console, to be understood as much as to understand, to be loved as much as to love. For it is in giving that we receive, it is in forgetting ourselves that we find ourselves, it is in forgiving that we are forgiven, and it is in dying that we are raised up into eternal life."

I know by experience that it is possible to pass from the demanding lust, miscalled love, to the awareness of ourselves by which we can learn to give love. Some years back I thought that I was deeply in love, but that love caused me much torment: I was constantly seeking reassurance from the other person, constantly wanting opportunities of meeting, resenting everything and everyone who came in the way of those meetings and then tormenting myself that I was not loved when there was silence on the phone or by letter—at last the demands became wearisome to the other, who did love me but found the love unable to bear the burden placed upon it and there was an open rift. Desolation, self-pity and loneliness followed, and I went to the Church to face this whole thing out in prayer. It was made clear to me that I was not really loving at all, I was simply wanting love to bolster up my own inadequacy: it was not the other person I cared for, but my own feelings, my own security, my own loneliness. I became aware of my motives, aware of myself, and in that awareness found release both for myself and for the other. I was able to release the hold, to give the freedom I had fought against, to see what my demands were doing to the one I loved, and I was able to do this with a new-found peace and with complete lack of possessiveness. Then I found that the very love which I had thought to be lost was given back to me, because the other found it to be no longer a slavery—I found that it is in giving that we receive.

The former Archdeacon of London (now the Archbiship of Perth), in an article in *Frontier*, Spring, 1963, says: "Mr. Williams's plea is for a deeper self-knowledge which will enable people to have the courage to be themselves as God meant them to be. In such self-knowledge, we shall be more aware of our true motives, and we shall have more of ourselves to give to other people, not only in the sex relationship, but in every situation and encounter. There is also the chance, nay, the confident hope, that in thus discovering our true selves we shall also find the temple where the Holy Spirit longs to dwell. And the awakened self will recognise the Divine Guest because deep down in us something akin to the divine nature is implanted. With God dwelling in us, our attitudes, feelings and actions will be moved by love, and, even if we err occasionally, we shall be forgiven because we love much."

It is the understanding of this kind of self-knowledge which must form the major part in our training of the young, so that they may see the difference between love and lust, so that they may be able to give significance to one another by deeper understanding of themselves, and of the situation in which they find themselves; and in that two-fold knowledge learn responsibility in all relationships. How we help them to such knowledge and responsibility must be our next concern.

THE TRAINING OF
YOUNG PEOPLE IN
PERSONAL RELATIONSHIPS

Three

When the prophet Ezekiel was asked to go and preach to the Israelites in captivity he said first, "I sat where they sat." This is always essential. In helping young people to understand themselves and their responsibilities in the situations in which they find themselves it is first necessary to sit where they sit; to understand for ourselves the pressures and environment in which they find themselves, and to help them to that understanding. Dr. Mark Abrams writes: "Adult society usually gets the adolescents it deserves: they can be grateful that more young people do not realise that they often fail to get the adults they deserve."

Never, perhaps, has there been an age in which

there has been more talk about young people. The subject has been a happy hunting ground for psychologists, sociologists, clergy and school-teachers, and has resulted in one of the most over-worked and emotive terms in the English lan-guage, the word "teenager"—never used until 1947.

Young people must sometimes get heartily fed-up with all the talk that goes on about youth, and which seems to vary between two attitudes, both of which show a complete lack of under-standing. The first is the attitude taken by many, especially among older people, that all young people are hooligans, delinquents and libertines obsessed with sex. The second is the complete reverse, which romanticises the younger genera-tion, speaks of them as a "grand bunch" who only need a little more understanding—there are no problems to be faced. Both of the attitudes are unrealistic. Modern youth is neither beyond re-demption nor beyond reproach, but simply a group facing the peculiar problems of their age and their world which either can mar them or which they can face and overcome.

It is well for us to remember that many of the problems of youth are common to every age. The Albemarle Report of 1958 says: "The attitudes of young people to-day give an impression that they couldn't care less, yet this attitude is not so much cynical as sceptical. They feel themselves in a world and society which disagrees about or is unsure about its meaning and purpose." This is true enough; but listen to Richard Hilary writing of the 1930's generation of youth (my own generation): "We were disillusioned and spoilt. The Press referred to us as the Lost Generation and we were not displeased. Superficially we were selfish and egocentric without any Holy Grail in whose search we could lose ourselves." If that is not sufficient let us see what Shakespeare, speaking through the mouth of the shepherd in *The Winter's Tale*, says of youth: "I would there were no age between sixteen and twenty-three or that youth would sleep out the rest, for there is nothing in the between but getting wenches with child, wronging the ancientry, stealing and fighting." Perhaps things haven't changed much in the centuries, after all, and the only consolation about being young is that time always heals it!

Nevertheless, apart from the perennial problems of adolescence, there are certain problems peculiar to this age which will affect their whole attitude to morality, and especially to traditional morality as it has been understood. As it is ex-

tremely important to understand how these background factors affect the way in which we shall
teach moral relationships, I am listing them in
order:

The effects of the age of affluence

Younger people today are for the most part
physically healthier and better looked after than
any previous generation. They have been born
and grown up since the last war, and they have
never known suffering or poverty. (I am speaking, of course, of the young people of the Western world, not of the East.) They have been
brought up on a materialistic philosophy of life
and encouraged to believe that what is wanted
can be bought. They have seen in their parents
often people whose highest standard of values is
"keeping up with the Joneses." They have seen
the wealth of material things which go into the
home bought on credit with the idea that immediate satisfaction is important. They have been
led by a complacent and vulgarist Government
to believe that "you've never had it so good" is
the best way to appeal to people.

So, from the earliest days, they are imbued
with the idea that anything is to be had if you
have enough money, and that anything you want
you should have when you want it. Is it sur-
prising, therefore, that they should in some cases
apply to sexual desires the same attitude of life
which their parents have applied to material possessions? If you want it you have it without too
much waiting. It is only the logical next step in
an attitude of life which has already been bred in
them by their parents. What is to blame for this
attitude but the materialistic attitude of society?
It is useless to attack the symptoms if we do not
get down to eradicating the cause of the
symptoms.

All the pressures of the advertising world have
been brought to bear to further this attitude to
life. Success is identified with glamour. The "pop
boys" are those who make the most money the
most easily. So "use this lip-stick; buy this cos-
metic; make yourself smell nice with this after-
shave lotion; style your hair this way or that way
and you will have all the sexual success you
desire"—such is the tenor of many advertisements. The glamour boy or girl becomes the
idol. To resist such advertising pressure is
bound to be difficult if you are daily surrounded

with it. To create the kind of person who can resist advertising pressure is probably one of the most important functions of education today!

Yet it is also an age without ideals and with few causes. It would be very difficult to say what are the basic ideals of Britain today or what are the causes to inspire young people. So often the television-ridden home, with mother at work and father not wanting to be bothered, results in a boredom which makes the beat-rhythm, the dance-throb, with its suggestion of the primitive, the most exciting and potent escape from the conventional boredom of many a home. As Carstairs says in the Reith Lectures: "Adolescents want to believe in something, and they lapse into cynicism only when there seems to be nothing to believe in. They are capable of acting generously and disinterestedly: for example I regard the teenagers' readiness to march in support of nuclear disarmament as an indication of their social responsibility."

The change in the conception of parenthood

The old heavy-handed father and mother have now gone; and they have been replaced so often by a mother who goes out to work and a father who sees himself rather in the role of an elder brother, anxious not to upset his children, and wanting only not to be disturbed. He has abdicated his responsibility and does not see himself as being there to give any special guidance to his children or to take seriously their discipline. Frequently it almost seems as though many parents have an inferiority complex towards their children; as though they are desperately afraid of being thought "square," and so assume a "broadminded" and "tolerant" attitude to the point of never giving advice at all. Frequently to the young teenager the home-life of his father and mother, especially among the middle-class, seems hopelessly dull, conventional and respectable, even if there are no tensions in the home; and the attitude of "we did not have that or do that in my young days" is treated as beneath contempt and old-fashioned.

The technological age

In an age where the emphasis is upon technology, nuclear power, space flight, etc., there will be an increasing respect paid to facts and what makes things work. This has its own effect upon morality and religion. It is widely assumed that religion does not deal with facts and does not really work, and that moral prohibitions and taboos which are the result of religious codes are irrelevant. Respect will be paid only to a moral basis of life which makes sense and will work.

The early onset of maturity and sexual freedom

Another factor which influences the outlook of young people today is the early growth of physical maturity (whether it is getting earlier as the years go by is a matter for debate) combined with the later age of school leaving. When a girl is often physically adult at 13 and a boy at 14, and the years stretch ahead of them before their emotional and mental maturity can catch up with their physical maturity, then this has several effects:

First, it makes them very uncertain of their status in society. They are conscious that they have grown up physically, but equally conscious that no one is willing to give them grown-up status in society. So there will be efforts made to be aggressive about one's adulthood. This causes a certain rudeness and aggressiveness, an attitude of "I'm no longer a child and will not be treated as one." It mean that things associated with adulthood will be taken up, which usually means the less-desirable features of adult indulgence like smoking, drinking, swearing, telling dirty stories and, of course, sexual promiscuity. These are signs of growing-up, so it is thought!

Secondly, it makes them join gangs, because that is the way in which they find sympathy in their difficulties, and fellow-sufferers who also want to express their independence. The gang strengthens their sense of independence and revolt—the hair-styles, flick-knives, 500-c.c. motor bikes, leather jackets are all expressions of that "toughness" which is the outward symbol to the adult world that "I am grown-up and not to be trifled with!"

Thirdly, it tends to lead to increasing sexual promiscuity and experimentation, especially in view of the lack of chaperoning and the freedom allowed to young people by many parents. (Many will allow parties to be held while they are away, sometimes even all-night parties.) Although many of the accusations of sexual promiscuity among young people are exaggerated generalisations, there is no doubt that there has been a considerable increase in venereal disease; and in 1958 over £15 million was spent by the state on children in care, most of them school-girl mothers. Quite often the boy-fathers are quite unrepentant, and the reply of a group of teenage boys when interviewed about this on television was, "Why shouldn't the state take care of the brats?"

Even though it is probably still only a small proportion of young people who are sexually promiscuous, there are many from eminently respectable homes who would see no harm in sexual intercourse with their "steady" girl-friend. In 1961 31% of the girls who got married while in their teens were pregnant at their wedding.

Of the present attitude to sexual relationships Professor Carstairs says in *This Island Now*:[1] "In a previous age children grew up in a community which had strong views of right and wrong; today, however, both the Church-going and the popular types of morality have tended to slip into disuse; popular morality is now a waste-land littered with the debris of broken convictions. Concepts such as honour and honesty have an old-fashioned sound, but nothing has taken their

place. The confusion is, perhaps, greatest over
sexual morality. Here the former theological
canons of behaviour are seldom taken seriously.
In their place a new concept is emerging of sexual
relationship as a source of pleasure, but also as
a mutual encountering of personalities in which
each explores the other and at the same time discovers new depths in himself or herself."

This, then, is the situation in which the training
in personal relationships must take place. From an
examination of this situation it will be seen why,
whether we like it or not, the traditional attitude
to morality is unlikely to be heeded. The apparent neglect of standards in the adult world
leads to a contempt for such standards. "If they
haven't worked for them, why should they think
they will work for us?" The reaction against
authority does not encourage the likelihood of
obedience to an authoritarian law. The attitude
towards the satisfaction of desires in the affluent
society is not likely to lead by law or code into
a different attitude towards sexual desires; and
the pressures of the advertisement world, the
cinema and theatre world, and the press, all reinforce this. The irrelevance, which is so often
and to so many the visual image of the Church,

is unlikely to cause such words as "sin," "morality," "duty" and "discipline" or "the Church condemns" to make much sense.

We may say that this ought not to be so; we may wish that it were not so; but nothing will alter the fact that it is so. It therefore becomes necessary that some other approach than that of traditional morality should be found if we wish to have any influence on young people today.

That other approach is the kind of approach which I have indicated as the approach of Christ; the approach of leading young people to the deepest and most profound knowledge of themselves; of helping them to a responsible and creative attitude towards life and people; of encouraging the right kind of revolt against conventionality, and of seeing them in the situation in which they are placed.

Let us now see how the forces of home and school and Church can help towards these four factors in helping young people to maturity. For maturity is what is desired, and maturity has been excellently defined as the quality of a person who shows a realistic grasp of his environment, a sense of conviction about his own purpose and identity in life, an ability to cope with everyday life and an ability to establish deep personal relationships with others, in which sex is not isolated but part of a whole.

Leading them to the deepest knowledge of themselves

Christ sought to do this by revealing to people what they were capable of, exposing the barriers and masks which they presented both to themselves and to society, and gently encouraging them to make the full and right use of their potentialities. This is surely the task of both home and school in relation to young people.

How can this be done? By the use of small groups meeting together with wise and experienced adults who will, without embarrassment or shock, help them to express themselves freely and help them to see what their difficulties are, why they are difficulties and what can be done positively about them. The greatest boon an adult can confer upon a young person is to show a real understanding of the difficulties caused by the gap between physical and social maturity, to be the kind of adult with whom they can "open up," and to give them the status of adults in conversation, showing that all problems will receive only wise and sympathetic understanding and not condemnation.

This can be achieved in various ways. In my own parish such adults who had the capacity to bridge the gap between adulthood and youth used to have little groups of boys and girls together to discuss quite freely the difficulties and tensions of personal relationships. "How far can you go?," "What is right for a steady?," "Is chastity important and if so, why?" Such discussions usually took place in the homes of the adults, in an informal setting and were a great boon and release to many a young person.

In one comprehensive school the headmaster said that the teaching of biological facts without teaching in personal relationships was worse than no teaching at all, and he has incorporated on to his staff people who are experienced in this kind of understanding, and gathered small groups together to investigate and examine the whole field of human relationships—again with tremendous benefit.

In both home and school and church there can be promoted the kind of conversation and discussion which can attempt to pierce through the superficialities of society, to reveal the shams of social convention for what they are, to help them to make the right choices in a world of abundance, to set them free from the chains of desire, of lust for things, of pride in possessions, and to help them bring to bear upon the problems of work, life and personal relationships the independent power of judgement which is free judgement. This can only be achieved by enabling the young to understand the means by which the pressures of society work and how they can best be resisted. The reading together of such a book as Vance Packard's *The Hidden Persuaders*,[2] for instance, would do a great deal to acquaint young people with the way in which advertising pressure works.

Help in understanding themselves and learning from the experience of those adults who have safely encountered sexual difficulties would extend to discussion of such things as "heavy petting," sexual stimulation as it affects different individuals, and the attitude of a boy and a girl towards sexual fulfilment. It is only when one realises one's own nature that one can know when temptation will become unbearable, and will be bound to mean a loss of control; so that the prayer "lead us not into temptation" will be understood, and those situations in which control becomes impossible may be avoided wisely.

Helping them towards creative responsibility

When a young person or indeed anyone begins to see himself in existence as a free being in the world, and begins to experience what that freedom means, he will begin to realise his own involvement in life and with others in life. It is only when we have begun really to love ourselves that we are truly aware of ourselves and our encounter with others. We cannot stand outside the world; we cannot be detached; we can only deal with problems as they affect individuals, and immediately we forget that we become involved in the kind of impersonalism which is so largely the evil of today—the impersonalism which views persons as units, as objects to be fitted into a scheme or a rule. This is a danger which besets all groupings, whether is be of state or Church.

In his work, *The Phenomenon of Man*,[3] Teilhard de Chardin shows how the development of human personality is the continuation of the "complexity-consciousness" which is the human end of the complex nature of the universe in the evolutionary process. Therefore the growth of a genuine community of persons combined with respect for the individual must be the next stage if progress is not to be retarded. This can only be achieved by a growth in love, not by a regard for rules. It is this kind of community consciousness, this sense of what involvement in life means in relationship to people, which must be the next step in their training. This will mean that, whether it is given in the home or the school, sex education will be a teaching not just of the functions and use of the body, but of the whole person in relation with other persons.

I would illustrate the kind of way in which this teaching may be given by relating a conversation I had a few months ago. I had been speaking to a group of Sixth-form boys at a public school about Christian morality and personal relationships. Afterwards, in individual discussion, one of the boys asked, "Why shouldn't I have sex with my steady girl-friend if she is willing?" to which I replied, "Tell me one thing first— when you say this girl is your steady girl-friend do you mean that you feel pretty certain that one day you will marry her?" He replied: "Oh, I wouldn't say that, exactly, but I like her, and she is quite agreeable." I did not answer his question for him, but put these questions: "Do you think you have a right to behave irresponsibly with someone who is not necessarily even to be your wife, and who, if things went wrong, would suffer far more than you, and if a virgin, might change her whole outlook? If you tell me that you love her, then I would say to you that sex is not isolated from love, but part of love and that, if you say you love someone, you care for her body, mind and spirit; you do not treat her as simply the instrument for your own desires. That would mean that you attach no value to her, and very little to yourself." We talked further, and I tried to show him what, in the context of personal responsibility and relationships, love meant. I told him that no one could really answer his question but himself, but that these were the kinds of questions he must be putting to himself. I have cited this story at some length because it illustrates the point that the mere quoting of a code or a law as a basis for conduct would have meant nothing; but speaking of conduct in relation to the whole sphere of personal relationship had at least given him pause to think more deeply about the whole question.

But this is a far deeper matter than merely giving an attitude towards problems of sexual relationship. The training which is needed is the right kind of training in relation to life as a whole. If the whole attitude of the home is merely a respect for convention or a regard for material satisfactions and "keeping up with the Joneses"; if the school gives the impression that spiritual training is unimportant, and that education is simply the amassing of facts in order to pass exams; if the whole attitude of the Church gives the impression of being terribly worried about sexual aberration but not at all worried about affluence, housing conditions and nuclear warfare; if "stuffy respectability" is to take the place of real religion—then, of course, the right-thinking youth will rebel, and the less-intelligent youth will simply absorb this philosophy of life, see that deep relationships are of no consequence and that all that matters is "getting on" and "status," and this will affect their personal as well as their public morality. Anyone who saw the film *Room at the Top* would see that the chief character's private sexual amorality was simply the reflection of his whole attitude to life.

This is where it seems to me the Church so often fails. It makes a great fuss and stir about private morality, but does not pay sufficient attention to the kind of purpose in the whole of life which governs all morality. It is the attitude that lies behind "you've never had it so good" that the Church should condemn, not just one aspect of its expression in the realm of sexual behaviour.

What, then, is needed? First, that the values of the home should be the right values, and that priority in outlook, conversation and action should be given to people and not things. Parents should have it brought home to them that it is in the ordinary conversation of the home and in the attitude towards life revealed in the home that values are learned. So often there is a great difference between the values professed and the values really held.

Recently at a Lay Training Conference a group of business executives from the Southwark Diocese were discussing a problem of business morality and integrity in relation to sales techniques, expense lunches, etc. Previously they had been studying in the Bible the story of Zaccheus. When discussing Zaccheus they had, as churchmen, all said the right things about values, money, success, etc.; but when it came to thinking of the kind of situation in the business world in which they were regularly involved they no longer said the "right" things, but talked about the real values of that business world, which were far removed from their "Christian" thinking. It is so easy to divide life almost unconsciously into two worlds—holding, on the one hand, the morality which we profess as Christians, and on the other, the morality of the world in which we live from Monday to Friday, which we accept and practise because it is how we "get on" in that world. If the young are to see that life is more than the satisfaction of desires, be they material or physical, it will largely be because the atmosphere of the home has planted in their minds the true values of life.

The school, however, will also play its part. The way in which the school assembly is conducted, and the way in which subjects are taught, will convey either the idea that religion is irrelevant and that there is no particular purpose to life or that there is a creative and responsible attitude to life which can be learned through both worship and teaching. If the teaching of the Bible tends to be purely historical and void of any personal act of participation, and gives an impoverished view of the Incarnation, then it will be no wonder if the verdict of the children is, as was revealed by one questionnaire, that "Jesus was a very good man who lived two thousand years ago and was put to death as a political prisoner; but what has He to do with the world of today?" Too often, a bad school assembly—consisting of a hymn, half-heartedly joined in, probably with bad words and a meaningless tune, a few quick prayers, a reading and then a volley of school announcements—conveys the impression that God is a trivial inconvenience, to be recognised and provided for, but disposed of as soon as possible so that the work of the school may carry on.

The best religious teaching is not through the separate teaching of religious instruction, but through each subject—whether it be history, biology, science, geography or English—taught as relevant to a purpose in life which is creative, and which brings involvement in the world and a responsible attitude to the life of the world. Thus, history will give us an understanding of the kind of world in which we live; biology will give an understanding of the purpose and right use of the body; science of the uses to which science can be put for the benefit of mankind; geography will be the means of showing the needs of underdeveloped countries, and the responsibility of the affluent West for their development; mathematics will show the need for exact thinking in relation to life, and so on.

I think the community as a whole has a responsibility to exercise such control over advertising and the press that the wrong values of life are not propagated for the young to absorb. Is there not great hypocrisy in a world where we allow the pressures of advertising to operate un-controlled and the press to have almost unlimited freedom Sunday by Sunday to conduct cam-paigns of "exposure of scandals and evils" which are only means by which the public may lap up all the worst incentives to lust, and yet make a great song and dance about the need to keep the moral laws? Recently, two Sunday newspapers gave great publicity to the sordid life-story and sexual depravities of an English society woman and to the private life of a prostitute. This sort of thing could never happen in a Russian news-paper; and it is an interesting reflection on the freedom of the Western world that its press standards are lower in this respect than those of the Communist world! If the Church wishes to conduct a campaign against immorality it would be better advised to turn its guns on those respon-sible for the purveying of such filth than on some of its own members who are trying to make sense of morality to young people in the world!

Encouraging the right kind of revolt

The questionings of young people today are often an indication not of irresponsibility but of the beginning of depth. It is because we, the

adults, have lived superficially, accepted superficial standards of worldly success, "keeping up
with the Joneses," accumulating material possessions, basking in conventionality and respectability, that many of the thinking young have lost
faith in us and see nothing in our kind of world.
Even the "beatnik" rebellion is a rebellion against
superficial conformity, although it so often loses
itself in a rather silly conformity of another kind
—to a glorification of dirtiness and untidiness in
appearance.

What we need is to encourage the questionings
of young people, to be with them in the attack
upon the shams and materialistic conventions of
society, and to help them to build a better standard of life in which the emphasis is upon the best
interests of the individual and the deepest understanding of life and of themselves. Revolt is
often right when the world is already "upside
down," and such revolt should not be discour-
aged but guided to the better ordering of life and
of society.

Seeing the situation through their eyes

The last point which I would wish to make in
the training of the young is that the moral advice

which is given must be cognisant of the situation
in which each person is placed. One of the essential differences between a legalistic system of
ethics and the attitude of Christ is that Christ does
not make flat judgements which are applicable at
all times and in all places, but existential judgements, where the individual can only grasp what
is right for him by understanding his own experience of himself and his own particular situation.

It is through concern and engagement with the
world and the circumstances in which he is
placed, and being utterly open to the claims of
love in that situation, that the right decision as
to conduct will be made. Here I would quote
from *Honest to God:* "Love alone, because, as
it were, it has a built-in moral compass, enabling
it to 'home' intuitively upon the deepest needs
of the other, can allow itself to be completely
directed by the situation. It alone can afford to
be utterly open to the situation, or rather to the
person in the situation . . . it is able to embrace
an ethic of radical responsiveness, meeting every
situation on its own merits with no prescriptive
laws."[4] In the words of Tillich: "Love alone can
transform itself according to the concrete demands of every individual and social situation
without losing its eternity and dignity and unconditional validity."[5]

This means that in relation to situations of sexual morality we need to train young people to that kind of responsiveness to the needs of themselves and of other people to know when it is right to give themselves and when it is right not to do so, and what kind of action should result from true self-giving.

Is pre-marital intercourse always a mistake? In the case of two young people who will ultimately marry I think that it is, not because of any code or law but because the situation is such that the utter self-giving will be possible of realisation and will be the greater in its fullness if all is not anticipated before marriage. And if there is not to be marriage, if it is simply a "steady" but "changeable steady," then the situation for the sake of each demands the withholding of such complete self-giving. On the other hand, I would agree with the Archdeacon of London, George Appleton (now Archbishop of Perth), when he says, "When two young people are much in love and instinctively give themselves to each other, is the sin as dreadful as respectable parents and clerical guardians of morality seem to think? Must the two, who have anticipated the fullness of love, for ever look back in shame on that self-giving? We can be sure that our Lord would look at them in understanding and love, and with

what foregiveness was necessary. Yet such antic-
ipation brings its own pain, particularly to the
woman, who needs the continuing tenderness and
companionship after the self-giving; and, once
awakened fully, loving sexual intercourse needs
continuance."[6] It is because of that last sentence
and the existential situation thereby implied that
we could counsel the waiting of such full self-
giving until it can have continuance in marriage,
although it is possible to conceive of situations
where such self-giving outside of marriage might
have to be judged in the light of all the circumstances rather than be met with outright condemnation.

It is in these ways that I would see our young
people trained to understand themselves, to behave responsibly, to have a creative attitude towards life and to deal with situations. It is in
this way, and in this way alone—not by law or
by regulation or by imposition of an authority
which will be ignored—that we shall train them
to realise that charity and chastity co-exist. It is
the training in what Tillich calls "a seeing love, a
knowing love, a love that looks into the depth of
our hearts"[7] that will enable them to accept for
themselves a morality which will make sense and
will work, not only in sexual affairs but in all the
moral decisions of daily life.

MARRIAGE: ITS MEANING
AND ITS FAILURE

Four

There is one sphere of life in which the code of a flat law, applicable to all and allowing of no exceptions, has left us high and dry in dealing with many individuals. This is when marriage has obviously completely and irreparably broken down.

*The present position of the Church
with regard to marriage and divorce*

The Church derives its present very definite teaching on the complete indissolubility of marriage from its interpretation of the sayings of our Lord, from the teachings of St. Paul and from

the general view of procreation as serving the
continuance of God's creation. It will be seen
that each one of these three is included in the
reasons for Christian marriage as outlined in the
beginning of the marriage service in the Prayer
Book. The words used by Christ as given in St.
Mark's Gospel are: "But from the beginning of
the creation, male and female made he them. For
this cause shall a man leave his father and mother
and shall cleave to his wife; and the twain shall
become one flesh: so that they are no more twain,
but one flesh. What therefore God hath joined
together, let no man put asunder." When further
questioned by his disciples Christ answered:
"Whosoever shall put away his wife, and marry
another, committeth adultery against her: and if
she herself shall put away her husband, and marry
another, she committeth adultery."[1] In St. Mat-
thew's version there is added to the latter part
the significant phrase "except for fornication,"
which seems to imply that this was the one
reason Christ gave for divorce. But there has
been much controversy as to whether this was
or was not a later interpolation. This remains an
unsolved question, but does not affect the general
tenor of the teaching. The great difficulty of
living up to this seems to have been recognised

immediately by the disciples, who replied, "If the case of the man is so with his wife, it is not expedient to marry"; to which Christ retorts, "All men cannot receive this saying, but they to whom it is given," presumably referring to the words of the disciples, since the words on voluntary celibacy follow.

As we have already seen, St. Paul regarded marriage as a safeguard against fornication for "such as have not the gift of continency," and this again is reflected in the marriage service: the causes for which matrimony was ordained are given as threefold—for the procreation of children, for a remedy against sin and for mutual help in life, in both prosperity and adversity. The absolute indissolubility of marriage is re-emphasised in the rest of the marriage service.

Nevertheless, despite these words of Christ, various branches of the Christian Church have interpreted them in various ways. The Orthodox Church recognises and accepts divorce on certain specified grounds. The Roman Catholic Church can disregard for its own purposes previous marriages and divorces of persons joining that Church which had taken place before they became its members, and can remarry them. The Free Churches will in certain circumstances remarry people after divorce. The Church of England is the strictest of all Churches in its absolute refusal to recognise divorce as a sufficient condition for remarriage. The main difference between the Church and the state seems to be that while the state also regards marriage as a lifelong contract, it yet recognises the possibility that some marriages can completely break down and makes provision for cases where this has happened; while the Church in fact refuses to recognise that any marriage can ever completely and finally break down.

This attitude results in certain very obvious difficulties. In the first place it means that even where, on all the existential evidence, a first marriage was a complete and disastrous failure and a second marriage has been a complete success, the Church must hold that the first marriage is the true one and the second is a sinful union. We may be compassionate with the partners to the second marriage and for all practical purposes recognise their marriage; but in theory we have to maintain that they are living in sin. In our dealings with the individual our practice and our theory conflict.

A practical illustration of this from my own experience as a priest brings out the strange confusion. A woman whom I knew as a regular member of the Church had been married some seventeen years previously with all the ceremonies of the Church. Three months after her marriage her husband had brought home to the house another woman, and continued to bring women home at various intervals for the next six months, forcing upon her every kind of ignominy and humiliation. At last her patience gave out and she divorced him. Two years later she remarried. She has now been very happily married for fifteen years, and has two well-cared-for children. Both she and her husband are regular members of the Church, and the quality of their home-life has been all that could be wished for in a Christian home.

According to the Church, her first marriage was the true marriage, her second marriage is living in sin. By any normal standards of reasoning, however, the first marriage was a tragic mistake and the second a true expression of "the twain shall be one flesh." The question is—can one maintain as a principle, in such a case as this, an attitude which conflicts with every evidence of human well-being and personal good relationships? There are many such cases. Are we happy to go on denying the validity of the second mar-

riage in the eyes of God, when, by its fruits, it is
a Christian marriage? I know it will be said that
hard cases make bad law, but we must learn to
recognise when the law has broken down, and
to judge cases not by the law but by the spirit.

A second difficulty is that as a Church we are
placed in the strangely ironic position of being
better able to deal with those who break our
laws and then come to us than with those who
ask our advice in advance. By which I mean that
when two people have actually remarried after
divorce, and wish then to enter into the life of
the Church, we know how to deal with them and
to show them true compassion; but if they are
Church people and ask our advice before enter-
ing upon divorce and remarriage we have nothing
to offer at all save the prospect of lifelong con-
tinence, however young they may be. This was
brought home to me very forcibly when a young
couple came to me after their marriage had completely broken down, with no prospect of reconciliation. They had married, when he was 20
and she 18, mainly from the desire to escape unhappy homes. Even their friends had advised
against their marriage, knowing that they were
incompatible; but with the stubborn obstinacy of
youth they had ignored the advice. After seven

years of marriage, in which each year brought increasing knowledge of their unsuitability to each other, they finally parted with no desire to be reconciled, for there was nothing left between them. Fortunately there were no children. Each of them came to me and said: "What does the Church expect us to do now—we are 27 and 25 respectively, do you consider it practicable that we, who have no calling to celibacy, can remain celibate for the rest of our lives just because we have made a failure of our marriage?" What could I reply? I had to reply that that was precisely what the Church did expect, but I knew in my heart that it was asking the impossible, with all their life before them. I found myself in the ironic position of wishing they had not asked me, but had gone ahead with their divorce and remarriage, then come back to me to know what they could do about their Church membership. Then I should have been able to help. As it was, I could hardly help at all!

Another problem arising from the present position is that it seems to involve the Church in an anomalous position regarding separation and divorce. We find ourselves saying that separation is possible, but not divorce; but, surely, separation—even if it keeps the letter of the law—de-

stroys the whole spirit of the indissolubility of
marriage. How can we talk of two people who
have been parted from each other for years as in
any real sense "one flesh"? Are they not in every
practical sense "put asunder"? How are they
fulfilling their marriage vows of "in sickness and
in health," etc.? How can they be in any sense
of the word "mutual society, help and comfort"?
Here it seems to me that for the sake of the law
we are making a mockery of marriage vows. The
Lambeth Conference of 1948 said: "We would
earnestly implore those whose marriages are unhappy to remain steadfastly to their marriage
vows." But how can one remain faithful except
in the letter when the whole spirit which under-
lay that faithfulness has departed? When there
is no union left of any kind save that of a legal
bond?

Then again, it involves the very difficult question of how far the Church has a right to influence legislation concerning marriage along the
lines of Christian principles when it is known
that many of those who marry do not accept the
Christian view of marriage. This applies even to
many who may go through the forms of marriage in a Christian Church.

This is illustrated by the attitude towards the

Bill promoted by Mr. Leo Abse, allowing for divorce to take place in certain circumstances after seven years' separation, and after all possible methods of reconciliation have been tried and failed. There is little doubt, from the inquiry conducted by *New Society* and by many others, that most people in our country would agree with this Bill; but the Church, through its leaders, feels compelled to bring every pressure to bear to block what a public opinion poll of the country might well support. This is ethically doubtful in a secular society. As Mr. Munby says: "It is one thing to hold a high view of Christian marriage; it is another to insist that this should be the law of the land. It is one thing within a Christian community to legislate in a particular way; it is another thing to advocate laws for all and sundry. A properly pluralist view of society ... might be ready to accept varying kinds of marriage in one society."[2]

The Church now finds itself in the invidious position of appearing to reject what would seem a sane and clean way of ending marriages which have obviously broken down, in favour of a way which makes of divorce a parading of moral offences in court, often a matter of collusion and hypocritical connivance, and a fixing upon chil-

dren of the stigma of illegitimacy. The objection
is that this introduces "divorce by consent," but
those who wish for a divorce by consent can, if
they are moderately careful, get it today. In
Australia and New Zealand there is provision for
divorce after separation, and this has not, in fact,
undermined the public attitude to marriage.

A re-look at Christian marriage and its meaning

This muddle of legalism into which we have
fallen as a Church has involved us in failing to
face up to the fact of the breakdown of marriage,
and has forced us to involve a secular society in
a so-called Christian view of marriage. All this
arises from the interpretation which is placed
upon the words of Christ: "the twain shall be
one flesh" and "whom God hath joined together
let no man put asunder." But what do those
words mean? Do they mean that when a form
of marriage has been undertaken and certain
sexual acts have taken place there exists a reality
which cannot be broken? Or do they mean the
reality of a relationship in which the twain are
indeed one, and in that oneness are truly joined

together by God? I would take you back to
Solovyev's definition of love: "The meaning and
worth of love consists in this, that it effectually
constrains us to acknowledge for another the unconditional significance of which we are conscious in ourselves." If this is love, then marriage
is the effective fusion of two existences into one.
"The twain shall be one flesh" becomes, as surely
as it is meant to be, "that "two shall become one
real being." Here marriage is the reflection of
that which is true of the whole of existence, for
true existence is to live in another as in oneself,
or to find in another the positive and unconditional completion of one's own being.

To be consciously married in this sense is to
possess within the orbit of one's existence a vivid
and pregnant analogy of our relationhip with
God. As Berdyaev says in *The Destiny of Man*:[3]
"The meaning and purpose of the union between
man and woman is to be found not in the continuation of the species or in its social import, but
in personality, in its striving for the completeness
and fulness of life and its longing for eternity"
(see also Solevyev's *The Meaning of Love*—the
best book that has ever been written on the subject). The true essence of marriage surely lies
in the quality of the relationship—"the twain

shall be one flesh." The unity made by God in their joining certainly could not have had reference merely to an outward form of words or a sexual act, but rather that two people each conscious of their own and each other's significance have united in the fulfilling of that significance in each other: so that such a union is created as really makes one being, each part completing the other, each part needing the other. These are the kind of unions that God has joined together. These cannot be put asunder because they have, in fact, become one. This *is* Christian marriage. When this union has broken down, when that sense of fulfilment has gone, when there is no longer completion but separation, no longer desire to be one, but desire to be two, then surely for all real purposes the marriage has ceased to exist as marriage.

But it may well be said that, while this is true in theory, few marriages can hope to live up to this high standard, and that even if the spirit of marriage has broken down, are we not driven back to a hard-and-fast code to keep the façade going? The answer is "No," partly because we cannot be driven back to that code. The whole attitude of society has changed, and whether we like it or not, the religious rules regarding marriage will not be accepted as hard and fast in all cases by any but a small fraction of society. Partly, too, because we have to ask ourselves what it is we are trying to preserve when the spirit of a marriage has gone. Are we trying to say that, for the sake of society, the façade, with all its burden of human misery and bitterness, must be maintained? Are we speaking for the children of the marriage (but is it happier for the children to grow up in a home from which love has disappeared?), or are we trying to maintain that something is indissoluble, when the whole evidence is that it has already been dissolved? I realise that there are difficulties is assessing each situation completely, but the deepest welfare of particular persons in a particular situation matters more than anything else in the world, and the façade of union when there is no longer union is merely a sham and pretence, a ghost of a reality now dead.

The maintaining of marriage

What, then, in the absence of rules and regulations, can be done to maintain the standard of happiness and stability in marriage? A *Sunday Times* inquiry of November 18th, 1962, said: "The old ideal of Christian marriage which still lingers in many people's minds—but not in fact—could be regained only by reversing the entire social progress of the last fifty years. Nor can we introduce a new, artificial a-religious code. But if we do without the rules we must make the learning easier. We should recognise how radically our values have changed; how they have moved, in our concept of the mutual responsibility of marriage, from rules to reason, and from duty to choice."

I would only partly agree with this. I would say that we must give the kind of training which will enable people to have understanding of what is true Christian marriage, held in being not by rules but by right relationships. What are the signs of these right relationships?

The mature individual is he who has the greatest knowledge of himself and, through this, sensitivity to the other person. This insight, both of myself and of another, is the converse of what a leading psychiatrist suggested was the major factor underlying cause of the break-up of marriages: "The biggest factor in marital disharmony is immaturity." This kind of immaturity is common knowledge to Marriage Guidance counsellors, who find that so many of their cases arise from people who have no understanding of themselves and why they act as they do. The words of Solovyev should help many who are puzzled because they can experience more than once the emotion of "being in love": "The problem of true love consists not in merely doing homage to the creature who is the object of love, but in seeing also that this creature is only one of many; then its unique significance for the lover may also be transient."[4] The consciousness of this would save many who find themselves in a triangular situation from rushing to a divorce court. Rather would they see that through the very pain and difficulty of this situation they may discover, or rediscover, the nature of that true love which seeks not to possess but to give.

Another test of maturity is the capacity to see that if the rules are to go, then they must be replaced by values of living which include a better outlook on life than concern for affluence, status and "I'm all right, Jack" social attitudes. Recently a torrent of sermonising came from the leaders of the Church about the moral state of the nation because a Cabinet Minister was involved with a prostitute. But this was rather like bolting the stable door when the horse had gone. It would have been far more to the point if the Church had launched a national campaign the moment the Government had appealed to the nation with the supreme slogan of selfishness, "You've never had it so good!" As Munby says, a secular society has limited aims, but, if even those limited aims are to be secured, it demands a people trained to recognise that they must live by higher standards than restricted selfishness. "The more choices men have to exercise, the more responsibility is thrust upon them. A secular society enlarges the area of men's choices, and calls men to greater maturity, as Bonhoeffer has made clear to us. Do men really want it? Can they bear it? It is surely the business of the organised Church and of all its members to help men to bear it, and not to call them back to childhood."[5]

Insisting on the observance of rules which have already been rejected is like calling men back to childhood. Training people who have accepted satisfactory relationships between individuals as the basis of morality means enabling them to recognise that such a basis must begin in self-knowledge and end in self-giving.

In regard to training in the understanding of

sexual relationships, which lie at the basis of happy and satisfactory marriage, this means removing the sense of guilt which has somehow pervaded the whole realm of sexual experience, so that to many the very idea of sex is sin and can only be made respectable in marriage. And even within marriage the "marital offence" which must be freely paraded in court when divorce is sought is the offence of adultery. As Solovyev points out, this has probably arisen from the idea that sex-love is simply a means to procreation, and thought of in any other way is sinful. But life is more complex than that. To deny the true emotional and physical significance of sex in society is to turn our backs on all the knowledge about man that the sociological and psychological sciences have given us. To deny the true pleasure and satisfaction which is not a subsidiary but an integral part of sex-love is to reduce the purposes of sex to that which is common to the lower animals. There often arises, because of this guilt-feeling, an obsession with sex leading to frigidity and frustration, to a conflict between what is thought to be conventional and what is actually practised.

The devastating revelations of the Kinsey report showed that what we so often preach about,

and denounce in public, we enthusiastically practise in private. We lie to one another about sex;
we lie to our children; and many of us undoubtedly lie to ourselves. But we cannot for
ever escape the fact that a sexually hypocritical
and guilt-ridden society produces the kind of
literature, films, plays and advertisements which
are preoccupied with sex; and produces, as a result, neurosis, perversion, psychosis, unsuccessful
marriage and suicide. We have to start teaching
that there is no essential conflict in the balanced
individual between the flesh and the spirit; that
sex is good and enjoyable if it serves the fulfilment of men as a total being. An American Professor of Religion, Dr. William Cole, has put it
thus strongly: "Sex is natural and good. It is
attitudes which are good or evil. In its efforts
to prevent irresponsible procreation Western
civilisation has used the device of what Freud
calls the walls of loathing, guilt and shame. . . .
The method of moralism has been weighed in the
balance and found wanting, partly because it
moves in the wrong direction, and partly because
it has based its case on fear."[6]

It is interesting to notice that in France, where
this sense of guilt in relation to sex is nothing like

so strong as in England and America, and where there has always prevailed a general view that sex is both good and desirable, there is less neurosis and less marriage breakdown. A permissive atmosphere of this kind promotes stable marriage just because it proceeds from true self-knowledge in regard to the vagaries and complexities of sexual feeling. The existence of such vagaries is accepted and does not wreck marriages, because there is greater understanding between husband and wife and greater acceptance of each other's occasional deviations.

Finally, there needs to be more training in self-knowledge with regard to the difficulties of middle-age: boredom and dullness sometimes come to marriage after many years when the children are no longer at home. The realisation that we are no longer as physically attractive as we were, leading often to a last desperate fling if someone younger notices us and flatters us; the deadening effect of settled habit and routine; the sense of failure in life—all these can lead to the breakdown of marriage relationships unless we learn to recognise them and accept them. If these difficulties come to us there are those able to help us to accept them—the Marriage Guidance Council, for example—and in their help to infuse new life into settled routine, then many a marriage difficulty in middle-life could be overcome. So often again it is the lack of self-knowledge, the lack of knowing where to turn for help, that leads to failure; and no amount of rules will keep alive what human inadequacy has killed.

Some practical lines of thought

These are some of the ways in which training is desperately needed. Apart from the training given in school and home already mentioned, we need to give encouragement to skilled help in marriage preparation and counselling.

The Marriage Guidance Council is doing splendid work in educating people to a sense of responsibility and true caring, both in preparation for marriage and in dealing with people whose marriages are in danger of breaking down. It seems to me one of the most valuable bodies working today, for it provides training in the meaning of responsibility and caring, and this by people who know that much more than law or code is necessary if the value of the individual is to be the chief concern in marriage. At present this body receives a minute Government grant. I would suggest that if the Church is really concerned to maintain marriage it should make the Government's life a misery until this work is adequately recognised and supported.

A great deal more care needs to be taken by both state and Church in marriage preparation. Courses of instruction should be obligatory for those about to be married, whether in a registry office or in church. A leading sociologist writes: "I would introduce divorce by consent, hedged round with delays which encourage reconciliation. I would make marriage more difficult. Require couples to register their engagement, then to wait a certain time before marrying."[7] This would make such proper instruction as I have envisaged possible for both Church and state.

A great responsibility rests upon the clergy to see that much more adequate instruction is given than at present. Not just half an hour in the study, but real training which involves understanding of responsibility and caring. Unless we are prepared to give priority to such training, we have no right to lay such stress on the indissolubility of marriage.

The breakdown of marriage

But what are we Christians to do when, despite all efforts, every possibility of reconciliation has been exhausted? What if the marriage has gone completely dead, and husband and wife have ceased in any real sense, save a technical one, to be "one flesh"? It is useless to go on insisting that what is dead must be made to look alive; that what is unreal must be made to appear real, and that any attempt to find another relationship which is conducive to true unity and happiness is completely to be forbidden. I cannot believe that this could be the attitude that Christ would have us take. It is completely out of keeping with His whole life and teaching. To insist on the literal following of the letter of the Biblical text in this respect, when in many others the Church pays only lip-service to the literal text, such as with regard to peace and war, the attention paid to wealth and influence and the giving up of possessions, seems the height of inconsistency. And it is not at all agreed that this is what the literal interpretation of the text means. The interpretation which I have suggested seems much more in keeping with the general tenor of Christ's teaching on relationship.

Certain courses of action lie open for further thought and action.

The Church, like the state, should recognise and do everything, by teaching and training, to maintain the marriage-state as a life-long partnership—and this for the sake of husband and wife, children and society. But again, like the state, the Church should frankly recognise when the marriage has ceased to be anything but a hollow shell of the promises made and the purpose for which it was intended. If it is felt desirable that such recognition should come from the Church rather than from the state (for why should the state end what the Church has begun?), then let there be Church courts which could investigate (for Christians) the reality of the breakdown, and then let there be some form of solemn annulment and absolution from vows, taken on the lines of the possibility of absolution from monastic vows. Is it beyond the capacity of the Church to judge for its own people in this way— presuming that it is only its own people who would ask for such recognition?

The Church should then reconsider the whole

meaning of Christian marriage in relation to its
rethinking on many other issues. Is it possible
that what is demanded is a greater extension of
the principle of nullity? The marriage which is
joined by God is indissoluble, but is every marriage which goes through the forms such a
marriage by intention and consent? If it has completely broken down might this not mean that
the essentials of the "one flesh" were never there,
and that it was never really a Christian marriage?
This would be difficult to prove, but many of the
Roman decrees of nullity are difficult to reconcile
with an exact following of the Biblical texts, and
can only be supported on a wider view of what
Christian marriage is. I do not know whether
this is possible, but it certainly needs consideration, and should not be ruled out as a means both
of safeguarding the stability of marriage and of
recognising when there is no true marriage
existing.

Again, whether the Church does or does not
recognise for itself the breakdown of marriage,
I do not think we have any right to bring pressure
to bear on society to insist that a minority view
of marriage should be reflected in the law of the
land.

The view of divorce held by the Church is not accepted by the great majority of the people. Mr. Abse's Bill would have made possible what the great majority would desire; that the "dirty scandal" should be taken out of divorce proceedings and that after seven years, when it is obvious that the marriage is dead, formal and legal recognition of that fact should be allowed without the necessity of proving adultery. By opposing this so rigorously the heads of the Churches have made it look as though the Church prefers the sordid to the decent way of ending marriage (I do not say this is justified, but this is the visual image given), and they have also made it look as though they are determined that a minority view should be enforced upon the nation. This is contrary to the whole principle of democracy, and as Mr. Munby says: "The Christian position [i.e. in a secular society] might even be ready to accept varying kinds of marriage in one society; this again would be no more than the acceptance of the realities of the world in which we live. There is far more variety in customs and actual behaviour in different parts of the country and among different social groups than is normally recognised. To say this is not to justify easy divorce on moral grounds, but rather to do justice to the actual ways in which people prefer to live."[8]

To conclude this chapter I would quote from *Honest to God:* "Love's casuistry must cut deeper and must be more searching, more demanding than anything required by the law, precisely because it goes to the heart of the individual personal situation!"[9] It is precisely the application of this casuistry of love which the Church needs today, both in organising training for the maintenance of marriage and in formally recognising when a marriage has ceased to be.

CONVENTION
OR COMPASSION:
THE MAKING OF
MORAL JUDGEMENTS

Five

In the last chapter of this book I want to show how the different kind of attitude towards morality which I have outlined will affect our standards of judgement of others. The great difference is between convention, which is born of the law, and compassion, which is born of the love of Christ.

The judgements of convention

Some little time ago a young woman who had borne an illegitimate child came to live in a

certain village. She had been the victim of much
unhappy gossip in the neighbourhood from
which she came, and so she had moved. Later
she moved again into my parish, and came to me
with her story.

"When I moved to that village I thought to
myself—I will join the Church, and there I know
that I shall find understanding and compassion;
for I had read in my Bible what Christ had said
to the woman taken in adultery. I went to the
Church and for a while all went well, but then
someone discovered that I was not married; and
immediately tongues began to wag. I found that
people avoided me. I asked the Vicar if I could
teach in the Sunday School, and he said that he
did not feel he could ask me because of what
people would say. After a while," she said, "I
knew that I should find no more freedom from
unkind talk in the Church than I had found in
the world outside."

This is a true story. It is typical of true stories
that can be repeated *ad nauseam* about the behaviour of Church people, and I am afraid repeated from within the Church community as
often as outside—perhaps more often. It is the
great contrast between convention and compassion; the contrast which Christ had to face many

times in His ministry. The Pharisees who brought that woman to Christ were acting in strict accordance with the law. There was a penalty for adultery, the penalty of stoning. They merely wished for approval for the convention. Instead they received a lesson in self-knowledge and compassion. The same regard for convention appears in the story of Simon the Pharisee, in whose house Christ was dining when the woman, who was a sinner, came to anoint His feet with the expensive ointment. "This man, if he were a prophet, would have known who and what manner of woman this is that toucheth him: for she is a sinner."[1] In other words, Christ ought to have known that this is the kind of person with whom one does not associate.

What a contrast in the attitude of Christ! He deals with people as they are. He loves them as they are. He sees with compassion what it means to be an outcast and an outsider from society, for He was in many ways regarded as just that. He sees what there is in each person to respect and admire. He knows that the woman taken in adultery needs encouragement, that she may be told to behave responsibly. He sees that the woman who anointed His feet had much love in

her, which has been misapplied, but is nevertheless characteristic of her true self. He reveals to
the critics the self-knowledge to which they
should have responded with compassion. Convention or regard for rule blinds men to these
things. Only love can be open to see how to
bring men to maturity through compassion.

The growth of convention

But the terrifying thing is that today the forces
which are making for conformity and convention
are growing. David Riesman, the American sociologist, has contrasted three types of moral
systems. Those which are tradition-centred;
those which are inner-directed, each man obey-
ing his own conscience and claiming direct access
to God; and those which are other-directed, in
which the individual subordinates his own values
to the expectations of the community around
him. The last he finds increasingly common in
modern society, causing a spiritual emptiness and
an impoverishment of personality. Kraemer and
Peter Berger have shown how the American
Church has become almost a sanctification of the
American way of life, an epitome of American

values and conventions. Has not the English Church too often become a sanctification of the English middle-class way of life?

The prize that our civilisation seems to hold most dear is respectability, keeping up appearances, subscribing to the values of the world around us. To reach the goal of respectability we must speak with the right accent, wear the right clothes, associate with the right kind of people and, above all, *not* be different! We must approve of the same things and the same standards of behaviour. To many, what the neighbours think is much more important that what Christ thinks. Even those who strive to be unconventional soon establish a new series of conventions.

For example, the "beatniks" who rebel against the clothes, the cleanliness and the morality of suburban respectability only become a cult themselves, in which the right clothes, the right attitude of cynicism and the right defiance must be shown—so that it becomes just another convention replacing a convention!

The fruits of convention

These become very apparent in the realm of moral judgements.

Often standards of judgement of right and wrong are made on entirely false premises. The mother whose main concern when her daughter gets into trouble is "What will the neighbours think?" is concerned with what is unimportant compared with the effect that all this will have upon her daughter. It means that we judge people not by their own intrinsic merits or personality but by their ability to conform. I remember that in one parish there was a family which was different from those in the rest of the road. They voted Labour when everyone else voted Conservative; they went on Aldermaston marches; the wife sat around on the floor on cushions instead of on a chair and wore striking coloured jeans. They were a devoted family, the parents were a good mother and father to their children, but the rest of the road said, "Yes, of course, they are all right, but just a bit odd. I wouldn't like to be too friendly with them." The attitude was one of slight suspicion. Why? Because they were just a bit different from the mass conformity, and the convention insisted that people should not be different! This is a relatively harmless example, but often such judgement can be very cruel towards those who are different. It is felt that they are undermining the security of

the rest, and the reaction is one of violent objection. Perhaps this is what is partly behind
the violent abuse that is poured upon homosexuals!

So today many people within the Church are
outraged by some of the thinking that has been
going on in Cambridge and in Southwark and
elsewhere. They do not see such thinking as an
exciting attempt to grapple with the problems of
modern secularism, to rethink in the present age
the meaning and message of Christ, but rather
as an undermining of their conventional thought,
to be resisted at all costs and with accusations of
heresy. So fear makes us condemn. It is the only
weapon we have. It may seem incredible now to
us that the Pharisees should have preferred to
keep the rigid rules of the Sabbath rather than to
see healing done; but is it so incredible? Is it not
the same spirit which felt that Christ was undermining the security of their laws?—as indeed, in
a sense, He was.

Convention leads to a diminishing of the personality rather than a freedom of the personality.
Today we need men and women who know how
to choose, who know how to judge for themselves, who can resist the pressures of conformity, of advertising, of the press. We need those

who will judge people as persons and not regi-
ment them into groups as Negroes, prostitutes,
Jews, communists, homosexuals—to see a Negro
as both a Negro and a person, a prostitute as also
a person whose capacity for love needs re-orien-
tating, but not just lumped into a group and dis-
missed accordingly, and so with the others. We
want people who will stand out in a crowd, not
those who will get lost in a crowd. We want
people who have learned for themselves what it
means to be a person and who are capable of
passing on that learning to others in their personal
relationships. We do not want the life which is
a facade, papering over the cracks to maintain
respectability. We do not want people who live
up to society's judgements, but who through self-
knowledge make their own mature judgements.
We want the compassion of Christ, not the moral
laws of the religious and respectable.

Compassion and its learning

Let us be quite clear that compassion is not
sentimentality. Nor is it without judgement; but
it is the judgement of love on love, as St. John of

the Cross put it. Compassion is the identification which we can make in suffering with those who are themselves lonely, frustrated, sinful, weary and hopeless. Compassion does not sit in judgement from above and from without; it sits in judgement with the beloved and the sufferer. How, then, shall we learn compassion and true moral judgements?

Certainly only by the fullest knowledge of the facts and of the individual. So often we condemn because we do not know the facts, or have not taken the trouble to verify what we see and hear. Simon thought he knew all the facts about the woman who anointed Christ. All he knew was that she was a prostitute. He knew nothing of her capacity for love. The Pharisees thought they knew all the facts of the woman taken in adultery. They knew she was an adulteress. They did not know that, despite this, she could make amends if someone would trust her and re-establish her self-respect.

I remember a terrible story which came to my ears. A small car stopped each night outside a house; a girl got out, a man drove off. This happened very regularly, and always it was late at night. Soon tongues began to wag. "Did you hear her come in again last night? I know it was late because I was putting the cat out. Mark you, it's no business of mine, but her husband is away at present, isn't he?" Now for the facts of that story. The girl was the wife of a man who had to travel abroad on constructional work. In his absence she had taken a job as a cashier at a small café in the town which kept open late. Frequently the owner of the café had driven her home when the last bus had gone. Nothing at all. But the tainted tongue had done its work. The girl heard the rumours: she knew her husband had a rather jealous disposition, and she worried herself sick lest he hear the rumours and think them true. In a moment of great depression she committed suicide. Murder was committed by a tongue which thought that it was upholding the conventions, but had no knowledge of the facts.

Before passing moral judgement on any individual we should be absolutely certain that we know the facts, that the disclosure of the facts is going to help rather than hurt, and that we are aware of the circumstances which lie behind the facts. So often murder is committed by a tongue, yet the murderer goes uncondemned and is probably admitted to Communion; whereas failure in chastity would be immediately censured by the Church.

Again, before we pass judgement, we need to know *ourselves*. So often we try to deceive ourselves. We persuade ourselves in our righteous indignation against some transgression of the moral law that we are acting for the highest motives, when in fact we may be acting from fear, from insecurity, from guilt or even from sheer self-excuse. Somerset Maugham says: "It is curious that our own offences should seem so much less heinous than the offences of others. I suppose the reason is that we know all the circumstances that have attended them and so manage to excuse in ourselves what we cannot excuse in others." If we are to make any moral judgements we must not only know the facts of the case but also understand what *ought* to be the case. But here is where self-knowledge becomes most important. So often our view of what ought to be the case is preconditioned by a certain class-judgement, political outlook or moral upbringing, so that we think we are judging impartially when in fact we are simply voicing the traditional outlook of the class to which we happen to belong.

Full knowledge of ourselves will make us aware of the mysterious tensions between what we are and what we ought to be. Williams, in his essay in *Soundings*, shows how we keep the unknown self locked up, refuse to recognise it, then become dissatisfied with the known self and its inadequacy, and so try to snatch worth, either by stealing from others or disapproving of others.

This is how convention often acts. It will not dare to acknowledge the savage, caged prisoner beneath the known self. It is afraid; so it attacks violently anyone who has given a little release to the self underneath. Violent denunciations do little more than reveal the insecurities which lie beneath the mask of conformity; the fear of what may lie in me if I do not repress it for myself and condemn it in others. If only we could learn to bring what lies beneath to the surface, look at it, accept it and then learn fulfilment from it, we should act more objectively and compassionately in relation to others.

Although Williams chooses some rather odd examples of release of the self both in *Soundings* and in *Objections to Christian Belief*, there is no doubt of the fundamental truth that the effort to make myself run true to form with what rule and convention demands may very well mean that I am trying to be what I, at heart, know I am not. Then I not only feel frustrated myself, but I respond with anger when I see what I really want to do being done by others. I somehow feel they have become free and I am still enslaved; but I do not know that the real evil to which I have become enslaved is the conformity to a pattern of behaviour which is not my real self.

This pattern of behaviour makes me accept as evil what others, not my real self, call evil, and so to be angry when someone else breaks through that pretence. "To toe the line to a prefabricated pattern of behaviour may be the very sin against the Holy Ghost. For the apparent goodness of such a submission is a disguise for evasion; a refusal to run the risk and incur the possible terror of discovering the real evil of which I am a slave; an evasion made possible by my accepting as evil and so giving up what the moral establishment dictates."[2]

If we truly loved ourselves, knew the full significance of ourselves, we should not then be in conflict with ourselves, and not feel the necessity to abuse and destroy and condemn others. The destruction is the destruction of what we know and hate in ourselves but will not allow to be accepted and made clear to us. As Tillich has rightly said, "He who is able to love himself is able to love others. He who has learnt to overcome self-contempt has overcome his contempt for others."[3]

By learning to accept others and to be accepted

In that fine book which should be read by
everyone, *Come Out the Wilderness*, the author
writes of the situation which confronted them in
East Harlem, where the moral code as known to
the respectable was not even considered, and he
says: "It means that we accept them exactly
where they are and as they are—judgement
seemed to be the traditional Church's first word
in East Harlem. It almost seemed as if the first
concern was not to bring the lost sheep home but
to keep the lost sheep out in case they impaired
the Church's reputation for respectability. And
when the Church realises that it has a greater desire for a respectable community than for a redeemed one it must also realise that its whole
attitude to morality and its whole conception of
the Gospel of Christ is being called in question.
So the approach by way of morality was rejected,
partly because it was useless, partly because it was
irrelevant, but above all because the pastors slow-
ly realised that morality often stood in stubborn
opposition to the Gospel . . . so the Body of
Christ, the Church, must accept those who drink,

use narcotics, steal, have out-of-wedlock experience of sex. The Church is set in the midst of the
world not to protect its life but to give its life
away, that men may know that God loves
them."[4] Would that the Church in England had
always remembered that fact, and that the organi-
sations had realised that by acceptance, not refusal, will men be redeemed. If the Mothers'
Union would open wide its doors to the unmarried mother, to the lonely woman, to the woman
struggling to make a success of a second marriage
when the first had failed, it would have more
chance of redeeming marriage and family life and
reclaiming the lost than by its policy of exclusion.
We do not exclude people from our church or-
ganisations for their lack of charity: should we
therefore exclude them for lack of chastity?
Which is the greater virtue?

But not only must we learn to accept people
as they are and not as we would wish them to
be; we must also learn to face acceptance for ourselves. This may sound strange, but it is often
difficult for us to accept our own forgiveness, our
own acceptance by God. We want to earn it, to
feel we have done something to deserve it, to fit
it into our pattern of good works and solid virtues, and we have to learn that we are just ac-

cepted; there are no claims we can make. Perhaps
this is something the disreputable can do more
easily than the respectable, and why the prostitute, the dying thief on the cross and the mean
old taxgatherer, Zaccheus, could find Christ
more easily than the Pharisees. They knew they
were accepted because they could not possibly
have merited anything by themselves. They had
no illusions about their claims. That is grace—
to experience acceptance, when we thought we
were separated and rejected: "you are accepted
by that which is greater than you, and the name
of which you do not know. Simply accept the
fact that you are accepted."[5] Tillich goes on to
say that it is in that acceptance that we find peace,
we find self-knowledge, we lose our self-hate,
and so we are able to accept others as they are,
knowing that we are accepted as we are and both
belong to the same ground of love. This is true
identification, the identification of the respectable
with the disreputable because both are accepted
and neither merits acceptance. So we can understand each other and be compassionate with each
other, because we realise that there is no law, no
standard by which one is justified and the other
condemned, but only the commonalty of separation from God, which is sin, and the finding of

acceptance by God, which is peace and grace and love. This is the freedom found in Christ, the morality which is above the law; the morality which is not even morality, but simply the working out of that love which is the ground of all our being, the love mirrored in Christ and now given to us to show forth in the same acceptance of His children.

By identification with those in need

It is by this acceptance that we learn the last lesson of compassion. Williams says: "We cannot bear to put ourselves in the same class with the afflicted." But to be compassionate at the deepest level we must. That is the secret of the Cross. That is what Christ did. He put Himself in the same class with the afflicted. He realised that only a suffering God can help, only a God who knows what it is to be weak, to be lonely, to be unwanted, to be ostracised. Unless we have done this, unless we have put ourselves into the very being and feeling of others in their moral difficulties we shall never be able to help them face and bear them; we shall never know to what

action our compassion should lead. Such is possible when we have learned that acceptance
which brings its own identification. Father Tal-
bot, in his *Retreat Addresses*, says: "I remember
a tragic event when a man fell from high estate
to great disgrace. The world sniggered. I saw
another great man and caught an insight into the
passion itself. He was twisted with agony for
love of this other man and I saw a little bit of
what the broken heart of faith, hope and love can
be—if we care." I thought of those words at the
time of the Profumo scandal, when everyone was
rushing in to preach sermons on morality and to
lay the blame at the feet of those who were pro-
claiming what is called the "new morality," as
though no statesman had ever previously in history led an immoral life!

Let our identification teach us what to do, as
that of many others has taught them; like the
nuns who read the *News of the World* for ago-
nised intercession; like the young man in Poplar
whose knowledge of old age and poverty led him
to establish the Teenage Friendship Society to
help and befriend them; like the efforts of Father
Williamson among the prostitutes of Cable
Street; like the man in Holland who saw the
tragedy of homosexuals and founded a club for

them where they could find acceptance and friendship. So shall we learn compassion through identification, identification through acceptance, acceptance through self-knowledge and self-knowledge through the need to know all the circumstances which surround actions. Then, and then only, can we judge, but it will be the judgement which is based upon acceptance; the judgement which longs that people shall be mature and responsible, because there lies full co-operation with Christ. To quote again from *Come Out the Wilderness:* "What was needed was an acceptance which loved them and held on to them and also a judgement whose demands treated them as men." A judgement which helps them to "become what they are"!

This is precisely what the so-called 'new' attitude to moral law sets out to do. In the light of the almost universal rejection of the code we ask ourselves these questions: Is what the Church is teaching the same as Christ taught? Is a moral standard based upon a sense of care and responsibility and acceptance in personal relationships not far better than one based on a legalism for all? Is it not far more in accord with the Christ of compassion, whose whole life and teaching was based not upon codes but upon people and the conviction that people mattered, and that people could only be dealt with in their situation and in the full knowledge of their circumstances? This is the path I have been tracing through various spheres of morality, and in relation to various sexual and moral difficulties of today. There are many more things to be said, many more loose ends to be tied up, but the question remains open for discussion—Is the Church right to go on adopting to an unheeding world the attitude— "We are right and everyone else is wrong"? Or will the Church be humble enough to go back to the Christ of Galilee, the Christ of the Cross, and test its teachings by His?

APPENDIX

THE PREDICAMENT OF
THE HOMOSEXUAL

In the sermons from which this book origi-
nated I made reference to the problem of homosexuality. I do not wish to enlarge on this subject
here, as there are many books written exclusively
on that theme, but I think that there are certain
questions which, on the lines of the argument of
this book, we should as Christians be putting to
ourselves in relation to the predicament of the
homosexual. I will simply state them here as
questions:

Should we not judge this kind of relationship
by its quality rather than its appearance? The
Quakers in their Essay said: "Surely it is the
nature and quality of a relationship that matters.

143

One must not judge it by its outward appearance,
but by its inner worth. Homosexual affection can
be as selfless as heterosexual affection, and therefore we cannot see that it is in some way morally
worse."[1] If we are to take the standpoint of
morality outlined in this book, surely this should
be our approach to the whole problem of the
homosexual.

Should there be, in a Christian community, the
passion and prejudice which there is in the discussion of this subject? Homosexuals are a minority
group, but a considerable one (it has been esti-
mated at about 10% of the nation), and they are
a persecuted minority. It has always been the
province of the Christian Church to concern itself with the problems of persecuted minorities.
Should not compassion, understanding and concern be equally shown here? Should not the
Church, for example, make an urgent move to
insist that Parliament implement the recommendations of the Wolfenden Report, as it has already some time back in Church Assembly debate approved of those recommendations? Thus,
we should pay more than lip service to the official
line we have already taken.

Should we not be careful to understand the
difference between a criminal act and an act

which some people may regard as immoral? There is no conceivable theological, practical or equitable reason why the law should penalise a man for what a woman may do with impunity— yet this is the way the law stands in relation to acts between consenting adult homosexuals!

Ought we not to be working towards the kind of society in which we can learn to accept the homosexual so that he does not have to hide behind a mask? I had many poignant letters, many from homosexuals and one from a woman who had herself been married for twenty years to a homosexual and who could yet write with great compassion, which reflected the sense of loneliness at never daring to admit to their own nature. One wrote (and his letter was typical of many): "If all men could be made to feel the loneliness, the bitterness and the resentment of having to live in a society that refuses to accept him, then justice would be done."

Is there any special reason why it should be impossible for a man to be able to say, "I am a homosexual," so that he may share the burden of this condition? Cannot society learn to accept that he may be unfortunate enough to have this nature, with its consequent deprivations of marriage and family, but that he may, nevertheless, be a decent individual with a high sense of personal relationships and a great capacity for love? The visual image held by the public is so largely based upon the corrupt homosexual, but there are equally many corrupt heterosexuals, and one does not judge the good by the standards of the bad.

What help can and should be given them by the Church to overcome their sense of isolation and help them to find their own deepest welfare in the situation in which they, through no fault of their own, find it impossible to achieve a normal heterosexual relationship?

These are some of the questions which we must be asking ourselves if we wish to train the homosexual also in responsible relationship, to help him or her to accept his or her own nature, and fulfil it so as to be a valuable and useful member of society.

NOTES

CHAPTER ONE

[1] *Soundings*, Cambridge University Press, 1962.

[2] *Objections to Christian Belief*, Lippincott, 1963.

[3] *Soundings, op. cit.*

[4] *Honest to God*, Westminster, 1963.

[5] *Towards a Quaker View of Sex*, The Society of Friends, 1963.

[6] *Romans* 7. 10, 11.

[7] William Barclay, *Flesh and Spirit*, S. C. M. Press.

[8] *Soundings, op. cit.*

[9] *The Bent World*, Oxford University Press, 1955.

[10] *Towards a Quaker View of Sex*, The Society of Friends, 1963.

[11] See D. M. MacKinnon's essay in *God, Sex and War*, Fontana, 1963.

[12] *Objections to Christian Belief, op. cit.*

[13] *New Society*, May 23, 1963.

[14] *Luke* 11. 39, 40.

[15] *John* 7. 19, 24.

[16] Tillich, *The Shaking of the Foundations*, Scribners, 1948.

[17] *John* 8. 36.

[18] *The Shaking of the Foundations, op. cit.*

CHAPTER TWO

[1] *The Idea of a Secular Society*, Oxford University Press, 1963.

[2] *Ibid.*

[3] See H. J. Blackham's Introduction to *Objections to Humanism*, Constable.

[4] Theology and Self-awareness, *Soundings, op. cit.*
[5] *The Meaning of Love*, International Universities Press, 1947.
[6] Edmund Wilson, *Eight Essays*, Anchor Books, 1954.
[7] S. H. Miller, *Great Realities*, Harper, 1955.
[8] Tournier, *Escape from Loneliness*, Westminster, 1962.
[9] *Soundings, op. cit.*

CHAPTER THREE

[1] G. M. Carstairs, *This Island Now*, Basic Books, 1963
[2] Vance Packard, *The Hidden Persuaders*, McKay, 1957.
[3] Pierre Teilhard de Chardin, *The Phenomenon of Man*, Harper, 1959.
[4] *Honest to God, op. cit.*
[5] Tillich, *The Protestant Era*, University of Chicago Press, 1948.
[6] *Frontier*, Spring, 1963.

CHAPTER FOUR

[1] *Mark* 10. 6-12.
[2] *The Idea of a Secular Society, op. cit.*
[3] *The Destiny of Man*, Harper, 1959.
[4] *The Meaning of Love, op. cit.*
[5] *The Idea of a Secular Society, op. cit.*
[6] William Cole, *The Bible and the World of Dr. Kinsey.*
[7] *Sunday Times*, London, November 18, 1962.
[8] *The Idea of a Secular Society, op. cit.*
[9] *Honest to God, op. cit.*

CHAPTER FIVE

[1] *Luke* 7. 39.
[2] *Objections to Christian Belief, op. cit.*
[3] *The Shaking of the Foundations, op. cit.*

[4] Bruce Kenrick, *Come Out the Wilderness*, Harper, 1962.

[5] *The Shaking of the Foundations, op. cit.*

APPENDIX

[1] *Towards a Quaker View of Sex, op. cit.*

FOR FURTHER
READING

*Books on Ethics in broad sympathy with
the outlook of this book*

BONHOEFFER, D., *Ethics*, Macmillan, 1955.

BRUNNER, EMIL, *The Divine Imperative*, Westminister, 1947.

CAMUS, A. (Tr. J. O'Brien), *The Fall*, Alfred A. Knopf, Inc., 1957.

CARPENTER, EDWARD F., *Commonsense about Christian Ethics*, Macmillan, 1962.

CARSTAIRS, G. M., *This Island Now* (Reith Lectures), Basic Books, 1963.

DIXON, W. M., *The Human Situation*, Oxford University Press, 1958.

FLETCHER, JOEPH, "The New Outlook in Christian Ethics," *Harvard Divinity Bulletin*, October, 1959.

MACKENZIE, JOHN G., *Guilt: Its Meaning and Significance*, Abingdon, 1963.

MACINTYRE, JOHN, *On the Love of God*, Harper, 1962.

MACKINNON, D. M., AND WILLIAMS, H. A., The first two essays in *Objections to Christian Belief*, Lippincott, 1963.

MCMURRAY, JOHN, *Persons in Relation*, Harper, 1961.

MARCEL, G., *The Philosophy of Existence*, Citadel, 1961.

RAMSEY, PAUL, *Basic Christian Ethics*, Charles Scribner's Sons, 1950.

ROBINSON, JOHN A. T., *Honest to God*, Westminster, 1963.

SITTLER, JOSEPH, *The Structure of Christian Ethics*, Louisiana State University Press, 1958.

TILLICH, PAUL, *The Protestant Era*, University of Chicago Press, 1948.

The Courage to Be, Yale University Press, 1952.

The Shaking of the Foundations, Charles Scribner's Sons, 1948.

VIDLER, ALEXANDER, ed., *Soundings* (Essays 4 & 9), Cambridge University Press, 1962.

Books on the nature of our society

CASSERLY, J. V. LANGMEAD, *The Bent World*, Oxford University Press, 1955.

CHARDIN, PIERRE TEILHARD DE, *The Phenomenon of Man*, Harper, 1959.

KENRICK, BRUCE, *Come Out the Wilderness*, Harper, 1962.

KINSEY, A. C., *Sexual Behavior in the Human Male*, W. B. Saunders Co., 1948.
Sexual Behavior in the Human Female, W. B. Saunders Co., 1953.

MUNBY, DENIS, *God and the Rich Society*, Oxford University Press, 1961.

PACKARD, VANCE, *The Hidden Persuaders*, McKay, 1957.

Books on the training of young people

BARNES, KENNETH C., *He and She*, Penguin, 1962.

GOTTLIEB, B. S., ed. Barbara Ker Wilson, *What a Boy Should Know about Sex, What a Girl Should Know about Sex*, Bobbs-Merrill, 1957.

LOUKES, HAROLD, *Readiness for Religion*, Pendle Hill, 1963.

ODLUM, D. M., *Journey through Adolescence*, Penguin, 1961.

WELTON, VIOLET, *Burning Coals of Fire*, Seabury, 1961.

Books on Homosexuality

WEST, D. J., *The Other Man*, Whiteside, 1955.

WESTWOOD, GORDON, *Society and the Homosexual*, Dutton, 1952.

WILDEBLOOD, PETER, *Against the Law*, Messner, 1959.

Books on Law and Ethics

ELLUL, JACQUES, *The Theological Foundations of Law*,
Doubleday, 1960.
HART, H. L. A., *The Concept of Law*, Oxford University
Press, 1961.
ST. JOHN-STEVAS, N., *Life, Death and the Law*, Indiana
University Press, 1961.

Books supporting the legalistic view of Ethics

MCLAGAN, W. G., *The Theological Frontier of Ethics*,
Humanities Press, 1957.
WINGREN, GUSTAF, *Theology and Conflict*, Muhlenberg
Press, 1961.

Other books of importance

NIBLETT, W. R., ed., *Christian Education in a Secular
Society*, Oxford University Press, 1960.

SOLOVYEV, V., *The Meaning of Love*, International University Press, 1947.

SUTTIE, *Origins of Love and Hate*, Julian Press, 1952.

TOURNIER, PAUL, *Escape from Loneliness*, Westminster, 1962.

DATE DUE

GAYLORD			PRINTED IN U.S.A.